Heritage
Studies
for Christian Schools

**Marilyn Elmer**

Consultants    Dr. Timothy Watson
               Miss Melva Heintz
               Mr. Edward Richards

Illustrated by    Roger Bruckner    Brian Johnson
                  Barbara Gladin    James McGinness
                  James Harris      Kathleen Pflug
                  Bruce Ink         Stephanie True

**Heritage Studies for Christian Schools®: Book 3**
Produced in cooperation with the Bob Jones University Department of History of the College of Arts and Science, the School of Education, and Bob Jones Elementary School.

ISBN 0-89084-098-9

© 1982, 1993 Bob Jones University Press
Greenville, South Carolina 29614

# Contents

This book is called a heritage studies book. Do you know what we mean by our heritage? Do you know why we study our heritage?

A person's heritage is everything that has had a part in making him: who he is, what he looks like, how he thinks, and what he does. We study our heritage to help us understand how the Lord has blessed us. It makes us more thankful. Studying our heritage also helps us understand about our country, our families, and about ourselves.

Look at these children. They are alike in two ways. Each one is a Christian and each one is an American. Do you know how a person becomes a Christian? Do you know how a person becomes an American?

In other ways these children are different. What are some ways that they are different? What are some things that have caused them to be different?

Bo Williams lives in a nice home in Florida. His father is a salesman, and his mother is a nurse. Bo stays with his grandmother when his parents both have to be away.

Bo was saved in a Bible Club. When he told his parents about Jesus, they became Christians too.

Faith Sugimoto lives in California in a small house near the ocean. Her parents moved there from Japan a few years before she was born. They were led to the Lord by a missionary while still in Japan. Faith was saved in school last year.

Faith's father works with computers. Her mother works part-time for a florist. Faith helps take care of her little brother.

Meet Robert Fairfax. He lives in a large house in Virginia. His family has owned their home for over two hundred years. Robert's parents became Christians just before they were married. Robert was saved when he was seven.

Mr. Fairfax owns a factory. Mrs. Fairfax does not work away from home. They have a housekeeper who helps do the housework.

This is Katie O'Connor. She lives in an apartment in Chicago. Her great-grandparents came from Ireland about 50 years ago. They were Roman Catholics. Katie and her parents became Christians last year when a neighbor told them how to be saved.

Katie's father is a policeman, and her mother is a secretary. Every day Katie helps her mother cook and clean.

We can learn something about our heritage from the Bible. God tells us in the Bible about Adam and Eve, the first man and woman on the earth. They were the great-great-great-, and many more greats, grandparents of us all. Do you remember that Adam and Eve disobeyed God? They became sinners.

Every person born into the world since then has been a sinner too. In this way, the heritage of every person is the same. But because God loves us and wants us to become members of His family, He sent His Son to die for our sins. "For God so loved the world, that he gave his only begotten Son, that whosoever believeth in him should not perish, but have everlasting life" (John 3:16).

We can also learn from the Bible why people speak different languages. Do you remember about the great Flood that God sent to destroy the wicked people? Do you remember about Noah and his family who were saved from that Flood? After Noah and his family left the ark, children were born and families grew.

As the years went by, there were more and more people. God commanded these people to scatter out over the earth. They did not want to obey. They decided to live close together. They even decided to build a tower that would reach heaven. God was not pleased with these people. He caused them to speak different languages. Then these people scattered out over the earth as God had told them to do.

We do not know when God caused people to have different colors of skin, hair, and eyes. We do know that whatever God does is right; so it is right that people are different in these ways. We also know that God loves each person just as much as every other person. God is pleased with any person who obeys Him. The color of a person's skin does not matter. It does not matter if the person is rich or poor, or big or little.

God planned that people should live in families. He said that fathers are to be the heads of the families. Mothers are to be a help to the fathers. The parents are to love and to care for the children, and to teach them what is right. The children are to honor and obey their parents. They are to learn from their parents so that they can have good families of their own when they are adults. This was what God wanted in the family of Adam and Eve. It is what He wants in our families today. How can you help make your family one that pleases God?

This book will help you learn about families in early America. They are a part of the heritage of every American. It is especially important for Christians to know about these early Americans. We can learn from them how God cared for people who went through many hard times in order to do what they believed the Bible said was right. We can also learn about the importance of working hard in order to be successful.

Steven has just accepted Jesus Christ as his Saviour. He knew that he was a sinner. He believed that Jesus died to pay for the sins of all the world. He asked God to forgive his sins and to make him one of His children. Now Steven is a Christian.

Are you a Christian? Do you know that you are going to heaven when you die?

# 1 Map Skills

The earth is the Lord's, and the fulness thereof; the world, and they that dwell therein (Psalm 24:1).

# Goals

1 I will be able to name the seven continents and locate them on a globe.

2 I will be able to name four oceans and locate them on a globe.

3 I will be able to locate the North and South Poles on a globe.

4 I will be able to read the key of a map.

5 I will be able to locate my own state on a map.

What is the longest trip you have ever taken? Where did you go? How long did it take? What did you see there?

Pretend that you spend all of your time traveling. Do you think you would be able to visit every place on earth?

On the next few pages you will learn about maps. We use maps when we take trips. We can also use maps to learn about places on the earth that we will never visit.

These children are learning about the earth. They are looking at a **globe**. A globe is a small model of the earth. It shows the land and the water that make up the earth.

Notice that the globe is not straight up and down on its stand. It is tilted. The globe is tilted because the earth is tilted in space.

The earth travels around the sun one time each year. It stays tilted in the same direction as it travels.

We call the large bodies of land **continents**. There are seven continents. Your teacher will show them to you on a globe.

North America

Europe

South America

Asia

Antarctica

Africa

Australia

Which continent is the largest?
Which continent is the smallest?

The largest bodies of water are called **oceans**. Your teacher will show you four oceans. They are the Atlantic Ocean, the Pacific Ocean, the Indian Ocean, and the Arctic Ocean.

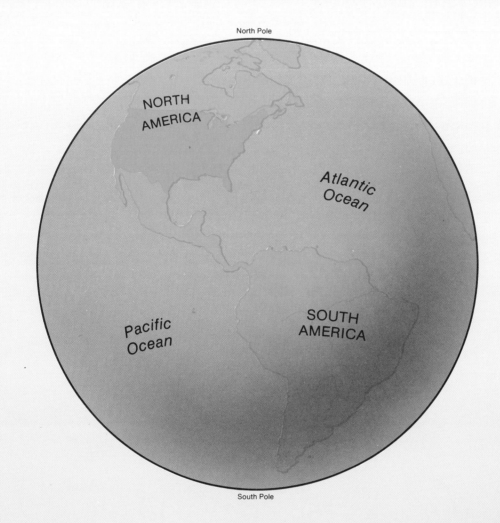

North Pole

NORTH
AMERICA

Atlantic
Ocean

Pacific
Ocean

SOUTH
AMERICA

South Pole

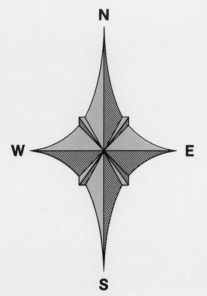

This map shows the continents and oceans on half of the earth. It is the half we live on. A half of the earth is called a **hemisphere**. This is the Western Hemisphere.

What are the two continents in the Western Hemisphere?

How many oceans can you find on this map? What are their names?

Find the United States on this map.

Find the North Pole on this map.

Notice the directions on this map. On most maps, north is toward the top of the map, and south is toward the bottom of the map.

What direction is toward the right side of the map?

What direction is toward the left side of the map?

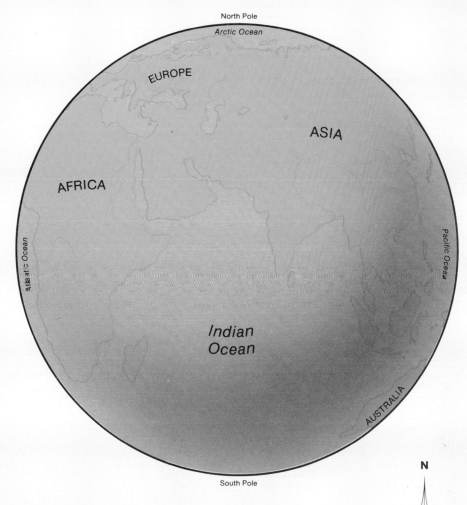

This map shows the Eastern Hemisphere. How many continents are shown on this map? What are they?

The maps on these pages show six continents. Look on a globe to find the seventh continent.

Find the Indian Ocean in the Eastern Hemisphere. Which oceans are in both hemispheres?

An **island** is a small body of land surrounded by water. Find some islands in the Eastern Hemisphere. Find some islands in the Western Hemisphere.

Do you see squiggly blue lines on the continents? These are **rivers**. All rivers run toward an ocean or some other large body of water. Use your finger to follow some rivers to the ocean. Can you find a river that runs east? west? north? south?

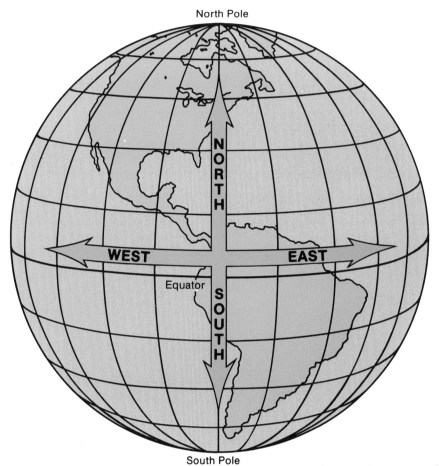

You can learn how to find directions on a globe. Your teacher will show you the North Pole and the South Pole on the globe. North is toward the North Pole. South is toward the South Pole.

There are lines on the globe that lead to the poles. If you use your finger to follow a line to the North Pole, your finger is moving north on the globe. If you follow a line to the South Pole, your finger is moving south on the globe.

There are lines on the globe that go left and right. When you put your finger on one of these lines and move it to the right, your finger is moving east on the globe. In what direction is your finger moving on the globe when it is moving to the left?

One line that goes left and right on the globe is called the **equator**. Can you find it in the picture at the top of the page?

10

What continent is shown on this map? Find our country. What country is north of the United States? What country is south of the United States? What ocean is east of the United States? What ocean is west of the United States?

Find the capital of our country. It is marked with this symbol: ✪ .

Find some rivers in the United States.

A **lake** is a body of water that is much smaller than an ocean. Find some lakes in the United States.

There are fifty states in the United States of America. Our country is called the *United* States because all fifty states work together to make one country. We have one government and one president.

12

Your teacher will give you a map like this one.
Follow these steps to show something about your
state.

1. Write the name of our country.
2. Find your state and write its name.
3. Draw a star to show where the capital of your
   state is located.
4. Place a dot to show your town.

United States
of America

0    100    200    300

scale in miles

Many maps have a **key**. The key tells what each symbol on the map means. Look at the symbols beside this map. What does each one mean? Find the symbol that shows the directions.

Columbia River

Sierra Nevada

Rocky Mountains

Great

Platte River

Plains

Arkansas River

Colorado River

Red

Yukon River

Alaska Range

0   100   200   300   400

scale in miles

1. What is the name of the mountains in the western part of the United States?
2. What is the name of the mountains in the eastern part of the United States?
3. The Mississippi River flows south into the Gulf of Mexico. What are three rivers that flow into the Mississippi River?
4. What are the names of the five Great Lakes?

**United States of America**

Lowlands

Highlands

Mountains

0   100   200   300

scale in miles

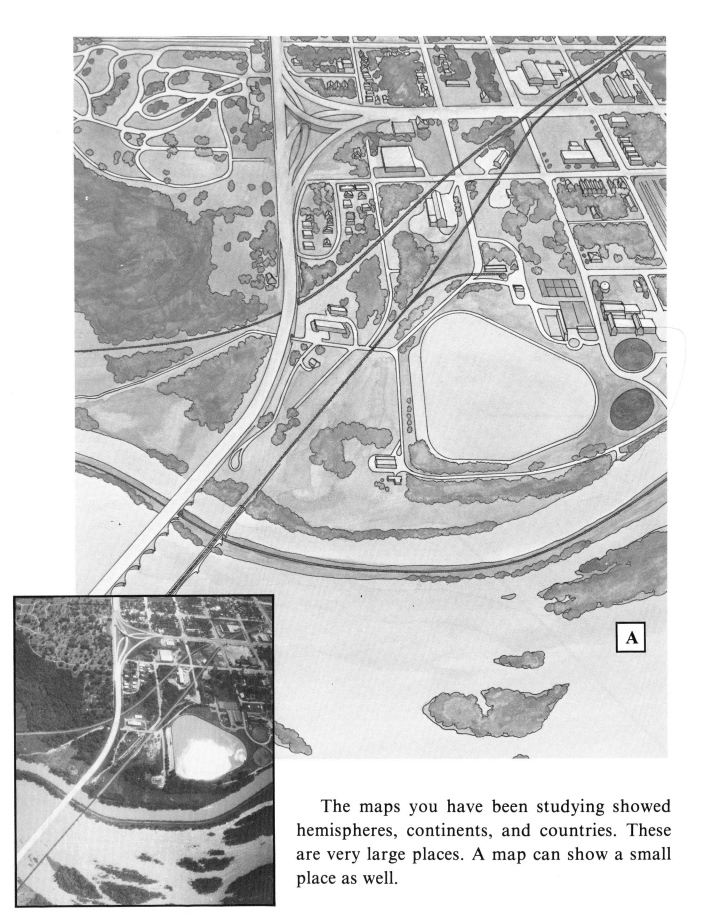

A

The maps you have been studying showed hemispheres, continents, and countries. These are very large places. A map can show a small place as well.

16

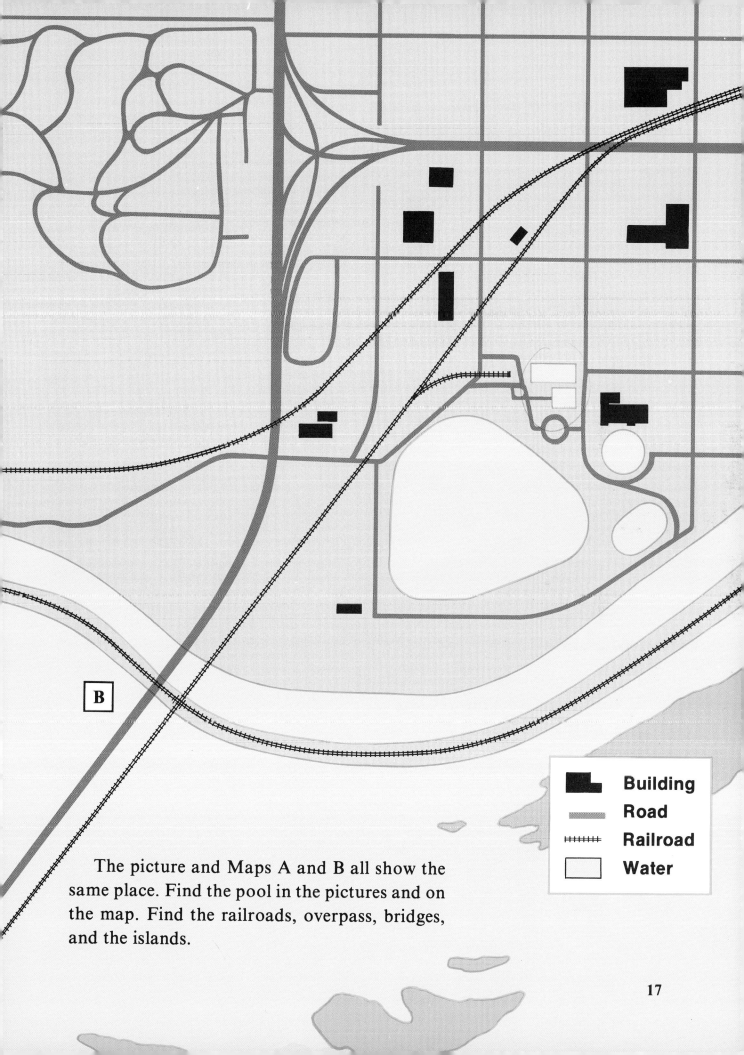

B

The picture and Maps A and B all show the same place. Find the pool in the pictures and on the map. Find the railroads, overpass, bridges, and the islands.

**Building**
**Road**
**Railroad**
**Water**

These children are making a map of their
school yard.

1. What color is the school building?
2. How many trees can you see?
3. Find the ball field.
4. What else can you find?


Perhaps you can make a map of your school
yard or classroom.

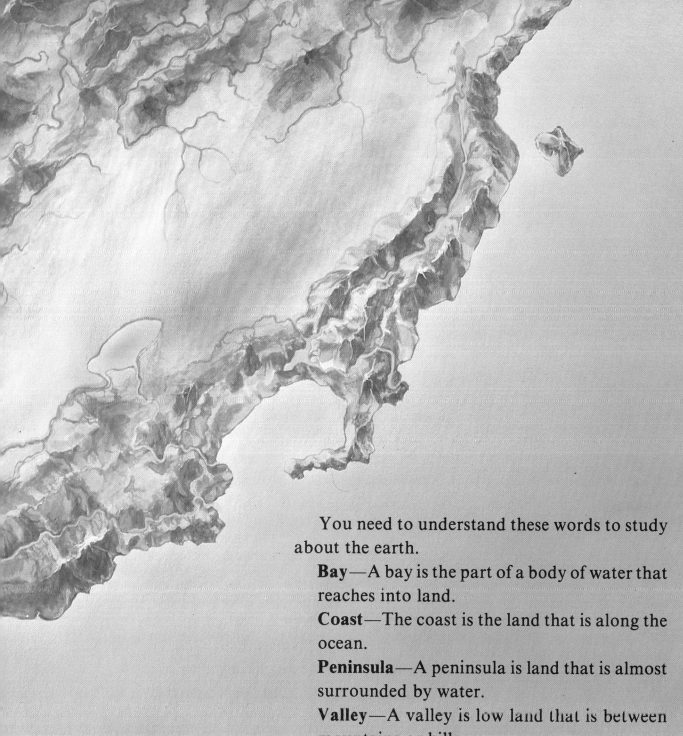

You need to understand these words to study about the earth.

**Bay**—A bay is the part of a body of water that reaches into land.

**Coast**—The coast is the land that is along the ocean.

**Peninsula**—A peninsula is land that is almost surrounded by water.

**Valley**—A valley is low land that is between mountains or hills.

Find examples of each of these words on the map at the top of the page.

Turn to the map on pages 14-15.
Find a peninsula.
Find a valley.
Find a bay.
Find an island.

One use of a map is to show us which way to go when we are on a trip. The Bible is our map to tell us which way to live while we are on our way to heaven.

Proverbs 22:6 tells us a child should be trained in the way he should go. Look for examples of good character as you study the rest of this book. Ask the Lord to help you make them a part of your life.

## New words

bay
coast
continent
equator
globe
hemisphere
island
key
lake
ocean
peninsula
river
valley

## Things to remember

Read each sentence. Choose the correct answer.

1. North America is a large body of land. It is a _____. (lake, continent, island)
2. A globe is a small model of the _____. (heavens, earth, sun)
3. The largest bodies of water are called _____. (rivers, lakes, oceans)
4. On a globe, south is toward _____. (the South Pole, South America, an ocean)
5. The United States is in the _____. (Eastern Hemisphere, Western Hemisphere)
6. A small body of land surrounded by water is _____. (a peninsula, a bay, an island)
7. In this book, ❂ is the symbol of _____. (the capital of our country, the largest state in the United States, the largest continent)
8. Alaska is the state that is farthest _____. (east, west, north, south)
9. On most maps, south is toward the _____. (top, bottom, left, right)
10. Land that is along an ocean is the _____. (bay, coast, island, valley)

**Things to do**

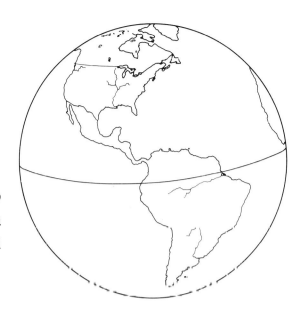

Trace this picture.
Put an *N* where the North Pole would be.
Put an *S* where the South Pole would be.
Find the equator. Put an *E* on the correct end to show which direction is toward east. Put a *W* on the correct end to show which direction is toward west.
Write *USA* on our country.
Label the Atlantic Ocean and the Pacific Ocean.

Look on page 7 to find the names of the continents. Write them in a list. Write the number of the picture on this page that matches each name.

# 2 The Indians

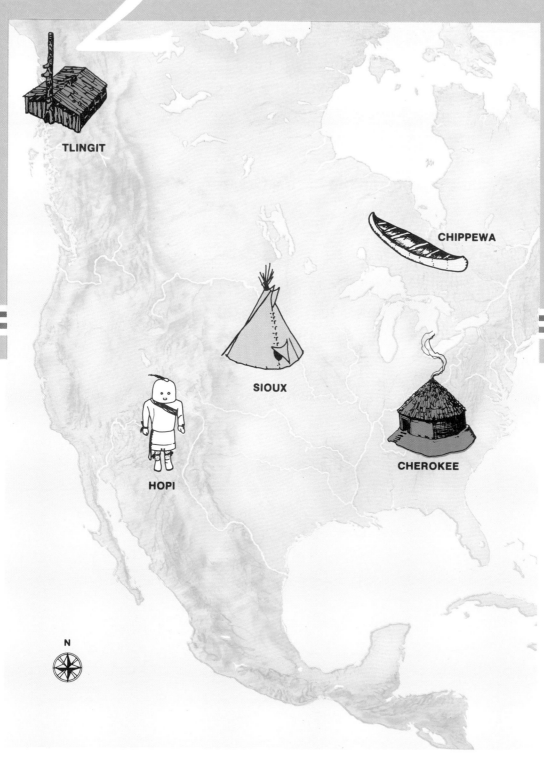

TLINGIT

CHIPPEWA

SIOUX

HOPI

CHEROKEE

N

*1* I will be able to tell how the Indians used their natural resources to provide their homes, food, and clothing.

*2* I will be able to draw pictures of Indian homes.

*3* I will be able to tell two things about the Indian religion that are different from the Christian religion.

*4* I will be able to tell some ways the Indians have had a part in the heritage of America.

*5* I will show by my life that I know what it means to be a good steward.

Have you ever wondered where the American Indians came from? Look on a globe to find where the Tower of Babel was built. (See page 2.) Use your finger to trace a path north and east across Asia. Notice that Asia comes very close to North America. We believe that long ago these continents were connected. When God confused the languages at Babel, groups of people probably traveled across this "land bridge" into North America. Perhaps people came to the American continents in boats.

After thousands of years, groups or **tribes** of people were scattered throughout North and South America. We call these groups of people Indians. The map on page 22 shows where some of these tribes of Indians lived.

The Indian tribes of North America were alike in several ways. The Indians looked very much alike. They had straight black hair and brown eyes. The men often painted themselves red, but they did not really have red skin. Their skin was brown. Most men did not have to shave because little or no hair grew on their faces. If a few hairs grew, they plucked them out.

The **roles** of the members of Indian families in most of the tribes were the same. The men were the hunters and the warriors. They provided meat for their families. They fought to protect their homes and their possessions. They also fought to show their courage and to get revenge on their enemies.

The women grew crops and prepared the food. They also made the clothing and cared for the children. They usually built the home as well.

Indian mothers took good care of their children. The babies spent most of their first year strapped to a cradle board. The mother or older sister would carry the baby on her back. Sometimes she would hang the cradle board on a nearby tree as she worked.

When the boys and girls were about six years old, they spent part of each day helping their parents or other members of the family. This is the way they learned the skills they would need when they were grown.

Indian children were taught to be brave and to endure hard things. They were not allowed to quarrel or fuss. They were punished when they cried. A lazy child was a disgrace to his family.

Indian children did not go to school. None of the tribes had a written language, so there was no need to learn to read and write.

When a boy was about eight, he had special training in hunting and fighting. What are some things a boy would have to learn to be a good hunter and a good warrior?

What are some things a girl would have to learn to be a good wife and mother?

*Indian longhouse*

When an Indian boy was about thirteen years old, he had to show that he was ready to become a man. He had an **initiation ceremony**.

Usually the boy went away by himself for three or four days. He would not eat anything during those days. We say that he **fasted**. Boys from some tribes spent the time lying on the ground inside a small hut. Boys from other tribes would lie out in the open or sit in a pit that had been dug for that purpose. If a boy was brave enough and strong enough to stay the required number of days, he was treated as an adult when he returned. Often there would be a special feast in his honor.

The boys of some tribes hoped to have a vision during their time of initiation. They hoped to see a spirit that would help them the rest of their lives.

Indian names sound very strange to us. The children in a family might be called Sweet Water, Gray Eyes, and Little Horse. The parents might be named Bright Cloud and Swift Runner. These would be their everyday names. Most Indians kept their real names secret. They thought that a person held a special power over them if he knew their real name.

Most of the Indian tribes had a leader called a chief. There was also a **tribal council**. This council was formed of the older members of the tribe who were respected for their wisdom. Sometimes women were on the council. The council gave advice to the chief when he had to make important decisions.

All Indians spent much of their time hunting, gathering, and preparing food. They ate the kinds of food they found in their **environment**. They ate birds, fish, and other animals. Nuts, roots, berries, and different plants were also used for food.

The Indians were the first people to grow corn. Nearly all the Indian tribes ate corn. It was often called **maize**. The corn that the early Indians grew did not look like the corn that we grow today. The ears were then about as big as a man's thumb and had only about fifty kernels on them. Later, Indians grew corn that had much bigger ears. The kernels of most of their corn were yellow. Some of them were red, blue, or purple. Indians even grew popcorn.

Look at the map on page 22. Notice the kinds of houses. The Indians made their houses from materials they found in their environment.

The Indians enjoyed listening to stories told by the older members of their tribe. Some of these stories, called **legends**, told about important events in their tribe's history. Other legends explained such things as how the world began and where animals and people came from.

The Indians did not have the Bible. Their religion was based on their legends. Since they did not know the truth about salvation, their religion was not true.

The Indians believed in good spirits and evil spirits. These spirits might be anywhere. They could be in the wind, in animals, in water, in clouds, or in trees. Most tribes believed in a Great Spirit who had created life. Dancing and feasting were important parts of their religious ceremonies.

The ideas of the Indians were very different from ours. They believed that the land belonged to everyone, even the animals. Everyone had a right to use the land, but no one owned any of it. Most tribes did not have any kind of money. Sometimes they traded with neighboring tribes, but they did not know anything about buying and selling. Often Indians took things from other Indians in different tribes. They did not think that this was wrong. It was expected.

The Indians and white people did not understand one another. Each group thought that its ways were right. They could not live together in peace because the white people did not agree that the land belonged to everyone. The white people put up fences and towns on the land that the Indians believed should be open and free to all.

## The Real People

The Cherokee was one of the largest Indian tribes in the southeastern part of North America. They called themselves "Real People." They lived in a land of mountains covered by forests. The Cherokee tribe was divided into towns of about five hundred persons each. They built a seven-sided temple in the center of each town.

The Cherokee had plenty of food most of the year. Many birds and animals lived in the forests. Fruits, nuts, and berries grew everywhere.

The Cherokee men hunted and fished to provide food for their families. They hunted deer with a bow and arrows. They killed birds and small animals with darts shot from a blowgun. They fished with a hook and line or a spear. Sometimes they caught fish in traps.

CHEROKEE

The Cherokee were good farmers. The men cleared the land, and the women planted the crops. They grew three kinds of corn. They also planted beans, squash, pumpkins, sunflowers, and tobacco.

The women and children gathered wild crab apples, persimmons, several kinds of berries, grapes, nuts, and other things to add to their food supply.

 The Cherokee Indians were careful in their use of **natural resources**. They did not like to waste things. They did not kill animals unless they needed them for food or clothing.

The Cherokee learned to make medicines from plants. One of their medicines contained a drug that is much like the aspirin we use today.

In the summer Cherokee Indians wore few clothes. In colder weather the men and boys wore leggings and sleeveless shirts. The women and girls wore skirts and capes. Everyone wore moccasins. The women made all these clothes from deerskin.

A Cherokee family often had two houses. The main house looked much like this picture. The walls were made of poles. Stems of cane plants were woven in and out among the poles. Wet clay was then spread over these canes. When the clay dried, it was much like plaster. The roof was covered with bark.

The other house was small. It was partly underground. It had a fire pit in the center and beds around the edge. The family slept inside it in the winter.

The Indians enjoyed playing games. The
Cherokee men played a game they called "little
brother to war." They were very serious about
this game. It was much like a game played today
called lacrosse. This game was played with a
small ball made of hair covered with skin. Each
player had two sticks with nets on the ends. They
used the sticks to get the ball through goals at the
ends of the field. The first team to make a certain
number of goals was the winner. They usually
played until one team got twelve goals. A game
often lasted for several hours.

This game was very rough. Each team had
from seventy-five to one hundred players. The
players used their sticks to hit the members of the
other team as well as to hit the ball. They also
kicked and tackled one another. Many players
were hurt during the game and some were even
killed.

*The Chippewa*

One of the largest tribes of Indians that lived in North America was the Chippewa, also called the Ojibwa. Find on the map the area where they lived. This land was covered with forests of oak, birch, and maple trees. Rivers ran through this land, and there were many lakes.

The Chippewa Indians' home was the forest. They went from place to place to gather food. Sometimes they walked quietly, in single file, among the trees. Often they traveled the rivers and lakes in birchbark canoes. Wherever the Indians went, the women built small huts called **wigwams**. The Indians slept in the wigwams, but their real home was the forest itself.

CHIPPEWA

33

The Chippewa ate a variety of food. The men hunted bear, elk, deer, moose, and other animals. They caught many kinds of fish. They even cut holes in the ice to fish in the winter.

A favorite food of everyone was wild blueberries. At the end of August the families traveled to the great patches of blueberries in the forest. They spent two or three weeks there gathering, eating, and drying the delicious berries. The dried ones were stored for winter.

The Indians then moved on to the shores of lakes to gather wild rice. This picture shows how it was done. Rice was one of the most important foods of the Chippewa because they did not stay in one place long enough to grow corn.

In early spring the Indians traveled to where the sugar maple trees grew. They made cuts in the trees and collected the sap that came out in birchbark containers. The women boiled it until it became maple sugar.

The Chippewa made all their clothes from animal skins. It took a long time for a woman to prepare a skin. She would first soak the skin in water for several days. Then she would scrape off the hair with a sharp stone or bone. Next, she would soak the skin overnight, stretch it on a frame, and scrape it again. This made it smooth and soft. Finally, she would tan the skin by placing it over smoking birchbark coals.

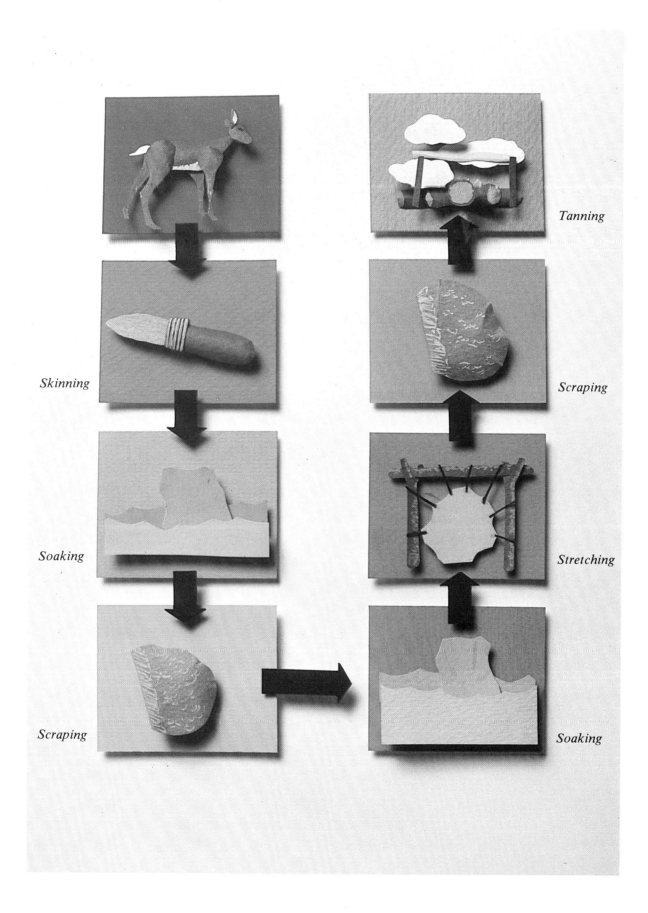

Skinning

Soaking

Scraping

Tanning

Scraping

Stretching

Soaking

35

# The Boy Who Became a Robin

Once there was an old man who had one son. The boy's name was Opeechee. The father was very proud of his son.

It was time for Opeechee to observe a fast before he became a man. He wanted to have a spirit who would be the guardian of his life.

The father wanted Opeechee to fast longer than any other boy. He said, "Opeechee, endure your hunger like a man. At the end of twelve days, you shall receive food and a blessing."

Every day his father visited Opeechee. Opeechee lay still and did not say a word.

On the ninth day, Opeechee said to his father, "Father, may I break my fast? I had a dream that spoke of evil."

"Fast three more days, my son, and you will be blessed."

On the eleventh day, Opeechee again asked to break his fast. His father said, "Fast another day, my son, and then you will be blessed."

On the twelfth day, the father again visited Opeechee. He found the boy standing. He had painted his chest red. He said, "My father would not let me break my fast. I will be happy because I obeyed my parent. My guardian spirit will give me a new body. Now I must go."

In an instant Opeechee was changed into a robin. He flew to a nearby tree. The father was very sad. Opeechee said to him, "Do not sorrow, my father. I will always be a friend to men and live near their dwellings. I will sing to make people happy."

Opeechee flew away. Since then there have been robins in the world.

## Indians of the Plains: The Sioux

The grassy **plains** in the center of North America were the home of several Indian tribes. One of these tribes was the Sioux. These plains were also the home of millions of buffalo. The Indians depended upon the buffalo for their food, for their homes, and for much of their clothing.

Buffalo meat was the main food of these Indians. Some was roasted or boiled. Much of the meat was cut into long strips and dried. This was stored to be eaten later. Some of the dried meat was pounded together with buffalo fat and chokecherries to make a food called **pemmican**.

Most of these Indians were not farmers, so they did not have corn to eat. Instead, they ate roots and leaves of wild plants. They also ate berries and chokecherries when they could find them.

SIOUX

The Indian tribes of the plains were on the move most of the time. They had to follow the buffalo herds. Their homes, called **teepees**, were made of buffalo hides draped over a frame of poles. The women prepared the hides and sewed them together. Designs were often painted on the teepees. The teepees could be put up and taken down very quickly. They were easy for the dogs to drag. The Indians did not have horses until the white men brought them from Europe.

The Indians used almost every part of the buffalo. Shirts, leggings, dresses, moccasins, and blankets were made from the tanned hides. Strings of rawhide were used to fasten stone heads to war clubs and arrow points to their shafts. Buffalo hair was woven into rope. Cups and spoons were made from buffalo horns. Ribs were made into sleds, and small bones were made into knives and other tools. The **tendons** were used for bowstrings and for thread.

The Indian tribes of the plains spoke different languages, but they had a sign language that all could understand. Here are some of the signs.

The Indian tribes of the plains often fought one another. The main purpose of the battles was to show the courage of the warriors. A warrior tried to touch an enemy with a spear, a bow, or even a stick he held in his hand. This was thought to require more courage than to kill an enemy by shooting an arrow from a distance. A feather was awarded for each brave act. When a warrior had enough feathers, he was allowed to wear them in a warbonnet.

Friend

Dog

Thank-you

**HOPI**

*The Peaceful Ones*

One of the most peaceful Indian tribes was the Hopi. The Hopi lived in the southwestern part of North America. This is desert country where there are many high, flat-topped, steep hills called **mesas**. The Hopi built their villages on the tops of these mesas. We call the villages **pueblos**.

The walls of a Hopi house were made of stones covered with clay. Poles were laid across the walls. Brush and grass were stuffed between the poles and covered with more clay. The door was often a hole in the roof. The men gathered the stones, and the women built the houses. The houses were joined together and looked like apartment buildings.

Corn was the main food of the Hopi. The men grew the corn in fields that were sometimes ten miles (sixteen kilometers) from their villages. Often the men dug irrigation ditches to provide water for their crops.

The women ground the corn into a fine meal and made it into a bread called **piki**. They mixed fine cornmeal and water to make a thin batter. Then they spread this batter by hand on a hot, greased stone. After cooking it a short time, they picked it up and quickly rolled it. When it was cool, it became crisp. The Hopi ate it by itself or dipped into a vegetable stew.

The Hopi ate very little meat, but they ate many kinds of plants that grew wild in the desert. The fruit of the cactus was a special treat.

Most of the Hopi Indians' clothes were made of cotton. It was the men's responsibility to provide their family's clothing and blankets. They planted and tended the cotton plants. They gathered the cotton and made it into thread. The men also did all the weaving.

In the winter the Hopi wore moccasins and robes of animal skins. They were usually made of rabbit skins.

The Hopi women spent much of their time weaving baskets and making pottery. Their work is some of the finest ever done.

The Hopi people believed in spirits they called **kachinas**. They thought that the kachinas helped and protected humans. At certain times, the men dressed up as kachinas. They wore kachina masks. When a man wore a kachina mask, he thought he had the power of that kachina. Sometimes the men wore their masks and visited the houses of the village to ask if the children had been good. If they had not, the kachinas punished them.

42

## The Tlingit

The Tlingit Indians lived along the northwestern coast of North America. They found that the weather was not very cold there even though they were far north of the equator. The nearby forests were full of animals, and the ocean was full of fish. It was easy for the Tlingit people to get food. They had time to do other things as well. They learned to make and decorate things. They were interested in becoming rich.

The salmon was the most important food of the Tlingit. Each spring these fish came to lay their eggs in the streams and rivers. The Tlingit men caught thousands of them in traps and in nets. They also speared them. The women cleaned and dried them. They could get enough fish to last all year in just a short time.

The Tlingit used a great deal of fish oil. This came from a small fish called a candlefish. They dipped almost everything they ate into this oil. They also used it in medicine and burned it for light.

These Indians also ate deer, elk, and other kinds of meat. The women had no trouble in finding berries, roots, and seaweed to add variety to their meals.

Most of the clothing that the Tlingit wore was made of deerskin. They nearly always went barefoot, even in winter.

The Tlingit depended on the forest for their homes. They lived in large houses made of cedarwood. The houses were built in rows beside a body of water. They always faced the water. Several families lived in each house.

TLINGIT

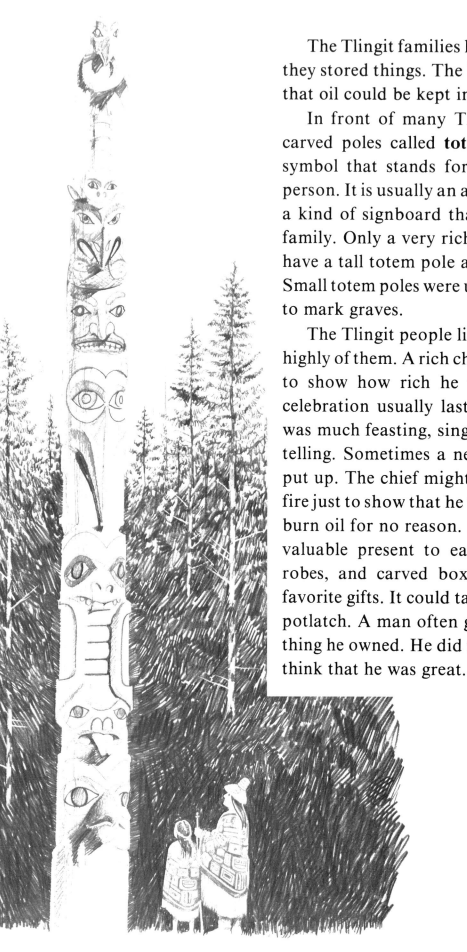

The Tlingit families had cedar boxes in which they stored things. The boxes were so well made that oil could be kept in them.

In front of many Tlingit houses were huge carved poles called **totem poles.** A **totem** is a symbol that stands for a tribe, a family, or a person. It is usually an animal. A totem pole was a kind of signboard that told about a person's family. Only a very rich person could afford to have a tall totem pole at the front of his house. Small totem poles were used to honor the dead or to mark graves.

The Tlingit people liked to have others think highly of them. A rich chief would give a **potlatch** to show how rich he was. A potlatch was a celebration usually lasting for ten days. There was much feasting, singing, dancing, and story-telling. Sometimes a new totem pole would be put up. The chief might pour a lot of oil on the fire just to show that he was so rich that he could burn oil for no reason. Finally, the chief gave a valuable present to each guest. Blankets, fur robes, and carved boxes full of fish oil were favorite gifts. It could take years to prepare for a potlatch. A man often gave away almost everything he owned. He did this so that others would think that he was great.

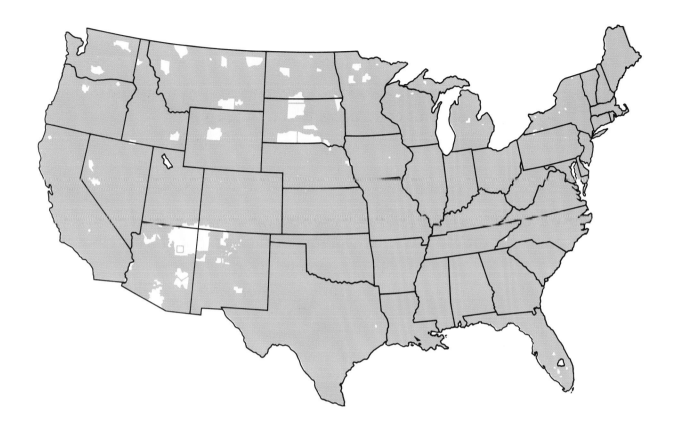

The yellow parts on this map show **Indian reservations**. An Indian reservation is a place where many Indian families make their homes. On reservations, some Indians live very much as their great-great-great-grandparents did.

The Indians have a part in the heritage of every American. The names of many rivers, lakes, cities, and states are Indian names. The words *moccasin, squash, chipmunk, skunk,* and *toboggan* are Indian words we still use today. Some of our highways are built where Indian trails used to be.

We do not know why God allowed the white people to take the land that was the home of the Indians for so long. We do know that God loves the Indians, and that they can become members of God's family if they accept Jesus Christ as their Saviour.

*Care for Property*

"And the Lord God took the man, and put him into the garden of Eden to dress it and to keep it."

Genesis 2:15

## New words

environment
fast
Indian reservation
initiation ceremony
kachina
legend
maize
mesa
natural resources
pemmican
piki
plains
potlatch
pueblo
role
teepee
tendon
totem
totem pole
tribal council
tribe
wigwam

## Things to remember

Write the name of the Indian tribe or tribes that fit each statement given.

Hopi    Chippewa    Tlingit
Cherokee    Sioux

_____ 1. They lived in teepees.

_____ 2. Their main food was corn.

_____ 3. They traveled in birchbark canoes.

_____ 4. They ate rice, blueberries, and maple sugar.

_____ 5. The women built wigwams.

_____ 6. Their main food was salmon.

_____ 7. They lived in pueblos.

_____ 8. Their main food was buffalo meat.

_____ 9. They carved totem poles.

_____ 10. They used sign language.

_____ 11. They wanted others to think they were great.

_____ 12. The men made clothing of cotton.

_____ 13. They built wooden houses by water.

_____ 14. They believed in kachinas.

_____ 15. They traveled most of the year.

## Things to talk about

1. Why did the different Indian tribes make their homes from different materials? Why did they eat different foods?
2. How were the roles of the Hopi men and women different from those of men and women in most Indian tribes?
3. If you had to belong to an Indian tribe, which would you choose? Why?
4. Did Indian children have more to learn than you do? Why do you think so?
5. Why is it better to learn about God from the Bible than from stories that are passed down from family to family?
6. Do you depend upon the environment as much as the Indians did? Why?

## Things to do

1. Pretend you are an Indian. Choose a name for yourself that "fits" you.
2. Make a teepee.
3. Make up a sign language for your class.
4. Draw a totem pole to represent your class.
5. Make a pair of moccasins.
6. List ten states that have Indian names.
7. Make piki bread.
8. Find out which Indian tribes once lived near your home.
9. Find out about missionaries who work on Indian reservations.
10. Draw pictures of Indian homes.
11. Write a legend.
12. Collect pictures of Indians.

# 3 The Explorers

# Goals

**1** I will be able to tell the reason that we remember the Vikings.

**2** I will be able to tell the reason that men wanted to find a water route to India and Cathay.

**3** I will be able to tell how America got its name.

**4** I will be able to locate the Saint Lawrence River, the Mississippi River, the Great Lakes, and the Gulf of Mexico on a map of North America.

**5** I will work to reach my goals.

Read the title of this unit. Notice the word **explorers**. Do you know what it means? The men you will be reading about came to America from Europe. Most of them were looking for adventure and for a way to become rich. They did not bring their families with them because they did not plan to stay. They traveled about to see what the land was like, and then they returned home. We call them explorers.

Have you ever wondered about the first white men who came to America? Who were they? Why did they come? No one is sure of the answers to those questions. This is what we think happened.

Find Norway on the map. Long, long ago the people of Norway were called Norsemen, or Northmen. They were tall people with blond hair and light-colored skin. The men of Norway were daring sailors. They built strong ships and sailed far from home. These brave sailors were called Vikings.

We do not know when the Vikings discovered the island that they called Iceland. The island is not really icy at all. Because the Vikings did not want other countries to send people there, they called it Iceland. Later the Vikings discovered another island. It was a cold island. There was very little land for growing crops, but the Vikings called it Greenland.

Find these islands on the map.

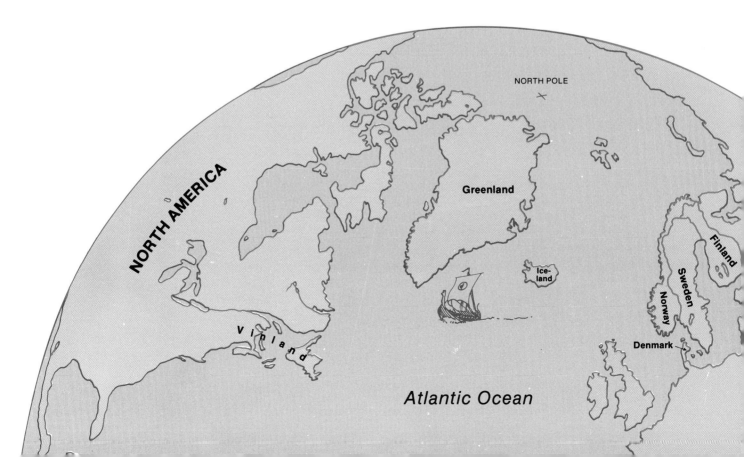

About a thousand years ago there lived a Viking named Eric the Red. He kept a diary. We learn this story from his diary.

Eric the Red had a son named Leif. Leif was a fearless ship captain. One time he planned a trip to Greenland. He and his men prepared for the trip. They sailed for days but did not see land. Weeks passed, but they still did not find Greenland. Finally, the weary sailors came to a place they had never seen before.

Some of the first things they noticed were the grapevines. They grew everywhere and were loaded with clusters of grapes. Leif decided to call the land Vinland, or Wine Land. Find Vinland on the map. Do you see that it is in North America?

The Vikings returned home. They told everyone about the new land they had found. The people then called Leif "Leif the Lucky."

The Vikings made many trips to explore the new land. They built small huts to live in while they were there. They met brown-skinned people who lived in Vinland. They learned to trade with them for furs.

We do not know why the Vikings did not move their families to the new land to live. We do not know why they did not build cities there. Perhaps the **natives** fought them and drove them away.

We do know that tools like the ones Norsemen used have been found in that part of North America. Ruins of small huts have been seen there. We think that the story about Leif the Lucky is true. We think that the Vikings were the first white people to come to our continent.

Hundreds of years went by. People in Europe built towns and cities. Travelers from Europe went to India and Cathay. (Cathay is now called China.) There they saw many wonderful sights. They saw rulers living in beautiful palaces decorated with gold and silver. They saw rich people wearing clothes made of silk and satin. They tasted delicious new foods flavored with spices. They learned about black stones (coal) that were used for fuel. They saw money made of paper.

The news about the riches in these countries caused many men to want to go there. People in Europe wanted to buy the spices, the rich clothing, and the jewels that were found there.

Find Europe, India, and Cathay on the map. In what direction did travelers from Europe go to reach India and Cathay?

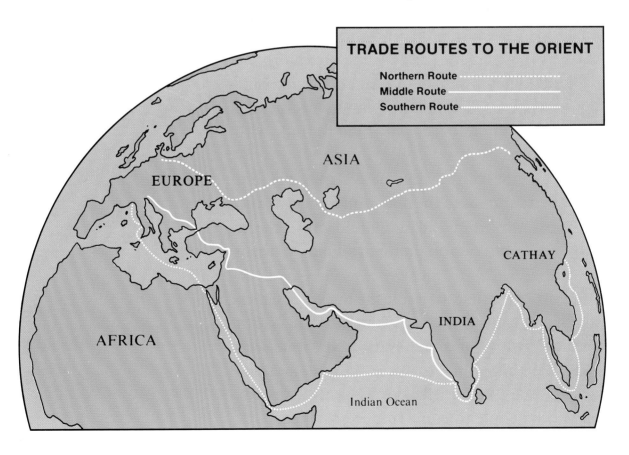

It was hard to travel to India and Cathay by land. The way was long. Part of the journey was through deserts. Part of the way was over high mountains. Travelers wished that they could go all the way to these countries by ship, but they were afraid to try.

Stories were told of great sea monsters that could swallow ships. Some sailors believed that the sea was boiling hot in some places. Some men even thought that a ship might sail right off the edge of the earth if it went too far from land.

Years went by. Schools were started to teach men how to make good maps. Shipbuilders learned to build fast ships. Someone discovered how to make a simple compass. Men learned that the earth was not flat, but round like a ball. But there was still much that they did not know.

Find some mistakes on this map. What continents are missing?

More and more people wanted to buy the good things that were brought from India. These goods were carried by camels until they reached the sea. The camel caravans had to pass through several countries on the way. The traders had to pay for the right to go through these countries. Then the traders had to charge high prices for their goods. Prices would not be lower until a way was found to go all the way to India by ship.

Some men thought that the best way to reach India was to sail around Africa. It was a long way, but they thought it could be done. Christopher Columbus had a different idea.

# Admiral of the Sea

The ship began sinking. A twenty-five-year-old weaver's son from Genoa, Italy, jumped overboard. Using an oar, he swam six miles to shore. He came to shore near Lisbon, Portugal.

Redheaded Christopher Columbus stayed in Lisbon. He lived with friends from Italy and worked with his younger brother, Bartholomew. They made maps and charts.

Columbus spent many days on the docks in Lisbon. He talked with men who had sailed down the African coast. He studied geography books.

One day Columbus had an idea. "Portuguese ships sail far to the south. Why can't they sail west around the earth's sphere? There must be land in that direction."

Columbus discovered that many ancient writers agreed with him. They wrote that the ocean between India and Spain was narrow.

In 1484, Columbus took his idea to the Portuguese king, John II.

"If you will supply the ships, I will reach the Indies by sailing west," Columbus said. For his trouble, he wanted titles of leadership. He also wanted a share of the riches.

The king's committee laughed. "The distance of such a trip would be too great. The world is much bigger than you imagine," they said.

King John II added, "Your price is too high."

"They will not stop me," Columbus whispered to himself.

.S.

.S. A .S.

X M y

Xp o FERENS

On May 1, 1486, Columbus met with Isabella, the queen of Spain.

Queen Isabella listened to Columbus. She gave his ideas to her committee. "Tell me, is the journey practical? Can the Crown afford it?" she asked the committee.

The Spanish committee argued for many years. Columbus thought they would never make up their minds.

Early in 1492, Columbus was called before the Spanish rulers, King Ferdinand and Queen Isabella.

"Your demands are too great," they said. "You are absolutely rejected. We will not help you."

Columbus saddled his mule. He packed his spare shirt, a world chart, and some books in his saddlebags. He left the court.

The king's treasurer was Columbus's friend. He spoke with the queen. "I am surprised that Your Highness will not risk just a little to gain so much. Another ruler may help him. That would be a great injury to Spain."

Queen Isabella thought a moment. "Call Columbus back," she said. "I will pledge my own jewels."

The treasurer bowed and said, "Very good, Your Highness. We will find the money. Your jewels will not be needed."

On Sunday evening, August 3, 1492, three ships left Spain: the *Niña,* the *Pinta,* and the *Santa Maria.* After years of waiting, Columbus's voyage had begun. But the sailors were afraid. As the days passed, the sailors grew restless and fearful. They grumbled and plotted together.

"We have already tempted God as much as we dare," said one man. "We have sailed farther from land than any other men have done."

The ship's steward spoke up. "We are running short of food, and the ships are leaking," he said.

"No one will blame us for deciding to return," said another sailor. "They will call us brave for sailing so far."

"Enough talk," the boatswain said. "If he won't turn back, we'll heave him overboard. We will say he fell in by accident while observing the stars."

Sometimes Columbus threatened to punish the grumblers. At other times he reminded them of the king and queen's reward to the first person to see land. But he always kept sailing; he never turned back.

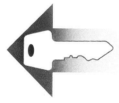

On October 11, an hour before moonrise, Columbus stood on the deck of the *Santa Maria*. In the distance, he saw a small light like a little wax candle. Was it really a light, or was it just his imagination?

At 2 A.M. the lookout on the *Pinta* saw a white sand cliff gleaming in the moonlight. He shouted, "Land! Land!"

It was October 12, 1492.

Later that morning, Columbus, his captains, and some of the crewmen went ashore in the longboats. The royal banners of the Spanish rulers flapped in the breeze.

Columbus and his men knelt on the white coral beach. They embraced the land with tears of joy. They gave thanks to God.

Columbus stood. "I name this island San Salvador," he said. "I take possession of it in the name of Ferdinand and Isabella. Those gathered here are my witnesses."

The seamen called Columbus by his new title—"Admiral." "We will obey you as one who represents Our Highnesses," they said. "We beg your pardon for the harm we have done you."

Columbus accepted their apologies. He pointed toward the green trees. Strange, painted natives peeked from behind the trees.

"I will win those Indians to Christ," said Columbus. "The gospel must be spread to all the earth. Who could be a better messenger than one who carries the name Christopher, the 'Christ-bearer'?"

The word *gospel* means good news. I Corinthians 15:1-4 tells us what the true gospel is. We do not know if Columbus understood this gospel or if he knew the Christ of the Bible. It is still important today that the good news of salvation through Jesus Christ be spread to all the earth. You can help to do this work.

Columbus and his men explored San Salvador and other islands nearby. They were greatly disappointed that they did not find gold or silver. They decided to return to Spain and tell about the land they had found. They took six Indians with them.

The king and queen were eager to hear about the voyage. They promised more ships and men for another journey.

Columbus made three more trips to the west. He discovered more islands. He made his brother Bartholomew the ruler of one of them. He died believing that he had found a new way to India.

Christopher Columbus made a mistake. He had not found a new way to India. He had done something much better. He had found a new part of the world.

The story of Columbus and his voyages spread rapidly. Now sailors were not afraid to sail far into the ocean. An Italian, Amerigo Vespucci, decided to make the same trip that Columbus had made. He realized that Columbus had been wrong.

Amerigo believed that the land Columbus had explored was part of a "new world." Amerigo wrote a book telling of his adventures and his ideas. He wrote, "A man sailing west from Europe must cross two oceans."

Later a man was making a new map of the world. The map showed the land between Europe and Asia. The mapmaker had read Amerigo's book. He decided to call the new land America.

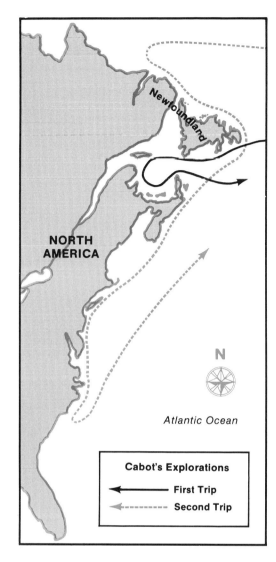

Cabot's Explorations

First Trip
Second Trip

Atlantic Ocean

The news of Columbus and his voyages caused great excitement in the countries of Europe. An Italian sailor named John Cabot lived in England. He went to the king with a plan.

Cabot thought that Columbus was right about reaching the east by sailing west, but he thought that Columbus had sailed too far to the south. Perhaps a waterway to India could be found by taking a northern route. The king agreed to provide a ship and men so that Cabot could see if he was right.

Look at the map to see where John Cabot sailed.

Cabot did not find a way to India. He did not find gold or silver. However, he did find rich fishing grounds. The king was pleased with Cabot's report of a "newe founde land." He said that all of this land belonged to England.

John Cabot and his men made another trip to Newfoundland. They sailed south along the coast, exploring as they went. We think that they went as far as what is now South Carolina before they returned to England.

As time passed, English fishing boats made many trips to the New World. But the fishermen did not stay here. They always returned home to England.

The king of France was disturbed. Sailors from Portugal had sailed around Africa to India. Spanish ships had traveled west and found islands that no one had seen before. The English king claimed that a new land his sailors had found belonged to England. France was being left out.

The king sent Jacques Cartier to America with instructions to find a way to sail to the eastern lands. Find his first trip on the map. He claimed that the land near these waters belonged to France. We call this land Canada.

On his second trip to America, Cartier found a great river that he thought might be the waterway he was looking for. It went in the right direction. He named the river the Saint Lawrence. Eagerly the Frenchmen sailed west. It was not long until the men's hope turned to disappointment. The river became narrow and full of rapids. They had to turn back.

Friendly Indians told the Frenchmen of another big river over the mountains. Cartier and his men returned to France. They told the king what they had seen and heard.

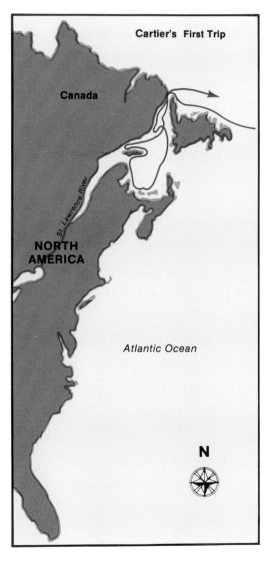

Many years went by. Robert La Salle was a brave Frenchman. He went to Canada to live. He heard the stories of the big river called the Mississippi. He decided to find that river and to follow it as far as it went.

La Salle went back to France to get help. King Louis the Fourteenth gave him permission to explore. Friends gave him money to buy supplies for the trip. He returned to Canada and soon was ready to begin.

The trip to the river was very difficult. The way was long. La Salle and his men were often cold and wet. Many times they were hungry. Indians were always near, and most of them were not friendly. Once La Salle and some of the men had to return to Canada to get more supplies. When they returned, La Salle found that some of the men he had left behind had been killed by Indians. The others had disappeared.

Finally they reached the big river. La Salle was excited as they went down the Mississippi. It grew wider and wider. This was the greatest river any of them had ever seen.

At last they reached the great body of water that we call the Gulf of Mexico. La Salle's dream had come true. He had traveled all the way down the Mississippi. He went to land and set up a tall pole. On the pole he put a sign that said that all the land along the Mississippi River belonged to France. He named the land Louisiana after his king.

René Robert
Cavelier Sieur de
La Salle

The explorers were searching for gold, silver, silks, and spices. Many of the explorers found only land. The land became the real treasure. The land became the land of new beginnings.

## Concentration on Goals

"But this one thing I do, forgetting those things which are behind, and reaching forth unto those things which are before, I press toward the mark for the prize of the high calling of God in Christ Jesus."

Philippians 3:13b-14

**New words**

explorer

native

**Things to remember**

Read each sentence. Choose the correct answer needed to fill in each blank.

1. The first white people to come to America were probably the _____. (English, Vikings, French)
2. Ferdinand and Isabella were rulers of _____. (Spain, France, England)
3. The largest ship that Columbus had on his first journey to the New World was the _____. (Niña, Pinta, Santa Maria)
4. When Columbus reached the New World, he thought he had reached _____. (Canada, England, India)
5. The great river that flows into the Gulf of Mexico is the _____. (Saint Lawrence, Mississippi, Nile)
6. Robert La Salle explored for the country of _____. (England, Spain, France)
7. John Cabot explored for the country of _____. (England, Spain, France)
8. Columbus explored for the country of _____. (England, Spain, France)
9. Cathay is now called _____. (India, China, Japan)
10. The title given to Columbus was _____. (Captain, Prince, Admiral)

## Things to talk about

1. Why did men want to go to India and Cathay by ship instead of by land?
2. How do you think the people of North America might be different if the Vikings had built cities and towns in Newfoundland?
3. Was Christopher Columbus a failure because he did not find a sea route to India? Why?
4. What are some dangers that the explorers in this unit faced? Why were they willing to face them?
5. If you could travel with one of the explorers in this unit, which one would you choose? Why?
6. What are some ways you can help spread the gospel of salvation to all the earth?

## Things to do

1. Make a list of spices that your mother uses in cooking.
2. Try to find out how silk cloth is made.
3. Use a globe and try to find a way to go all the way around the earth by ship. Start and end at New York.
4. Try to find what language is spoken on the island where Columbus first landed.
5. Plan a route around your school yard. Write directions for a friend to follow. Use a compass.
6. Collect pictures of sailing ships.
7. Draw a picture of a Viking ship.

# 4 The New England Colonies

## Goals

1 I will be able to explain what a colony is.
2 I will be able to tell how Plymouth and Boston were started.
3 I will be able to describe the first Thanksgiving.
4 I will be able to tell why people came to America.
5 I will be able to tell about life in the New England Colonies.
6 I will obey the commands found in God's Word.

Many people listened to the explorers' stories about the New World. They wondered if it would be possible to live there. Some thought of adventure or the gold and silver they might find. Some wanted a home where they could be free from the unfair laws of their own lands. Some wanted to be free to worship God in their own way.

It took a great deal of time, money, and work to get ready to go to the New World, but many men did it. They made plans to build homes, grow crops for food, and start businesses. They took their families and went to America to stay. They were citizens of their old country, but they lived in America. We say that these people started a **colony**. They were **colonists**. We often call these people **settlers** because they settled in America and did not go back to their old homes.

*Plymouth, Massachusetts*

On November 20, 1620, a small ship called the *Mayflower* came near Cape Cod on the shore of North America. Land was a welcome sight to the 103 passengers on the *Mayflower*. For two terrible months they had been traveling from England. The ship was very crowded. The only food was dried fish and meat, cheese, and hard bread. The weather was cold, and there had been fierce storms.

Even though the voyage across the Atlantic had been extremely hard, only two persons died. The first was a sailor. This man was not a Christian, and he mocked the colonists whenever he could. He told them that he looked forward to the time when some of them would die so that he could throw them overboard. One day the sailor suddenly fell sick. He had a very high fever. The next day he died. The other sailors on the ship did not mock the colonists after that.

Each person on the *Mayflower* was given a spoonful of lemon juice each day. The juice was to keep them from getting a disease called **scurvy**. No one liked the taste of the juice. One young man refused to drink any of the bitter liquid. He, too, died before the journey was over.

*The Pilgrims landing in the New World*

The passengers on the *Mayflower* were people who were looking for a home where they could worship God in a way that seemed right to them. We call them Pilgrims. A **pilgrim** is a person who travels far from home. Two of the Pilgrim leaders were William Brewster and William Bradford. A soldier named Miles Standish also helped lead and protect the people.

The Pilgrims knew that a colony must have laws. They asked God for wisdom to make good laws. The leaders wrote a set of laws for the colony. Each man signed them to show that he agreed to obey them. These laws were called the **Mayflower Compact**.

The people lived on the ship at first. The men spent several weeks exploring the land. At last they found a good place to build a town. The men built small houses and a fort. The fort was used as a church. They named their settlement Plymouth after a city in England.

The first winter was hard. Nearly everyone was sick and many died.

One day an Indian walked into Plymouth. He spoke English. He said his name was Samoset. He had learned to speak English from some fishermen who came to fish near his home far to the north. Samoset told the Pilgrims about an Indian chief who lived about forty miles away.

A few days later Samoset came again. He brought an Indian named Squanto with him. Squanto also spoke English. They said that the Indian chief Massasoit was coming.

The Pilgrims wanted peace with the Indians. They welcomed the chief and the sixty warriors who came with him. Samoset and Squanto helped the Indian chief and the Pilgrim leaders make a plan to keep peace.

Squanto came to live with the Pilgrims. He helped them in many ways. He showed them how to plant corn. He showed them how to catch fish. He helped them trade with the nearby Indian tribes. The Pilgrims thanked God for sending Squanto to live with them.

*Massasoit*

*Early colonists going to church*

The Pilgrims worked hard the first summer and raised a good crop of corn. When the harvest was finished, William Brewster suggested that they have a special day to thank God for His blessings. The people agreed. They decided to invite the Indian chief to a dinner on the same day.

The women began to prepare the food. They roasted wild turkeys, ducks, and geese. They cooked fish, vegetables, and dried berries. They made cornbread and pudding. The Indian chief and ninety warriors came. They shot five deer and many turkeys to add to the feast.

Thanksgiving Day was a wonderful day. Captain Standish and the men marched to the sound of trumpets and drums. The Indians and the Pilgrims had contests and played games. Before the feasting began, William Brewster led the people in thanking God for His love and care. They had suffered sickness, sorrow, and hard times, but they were free. They could worship God as they wished.

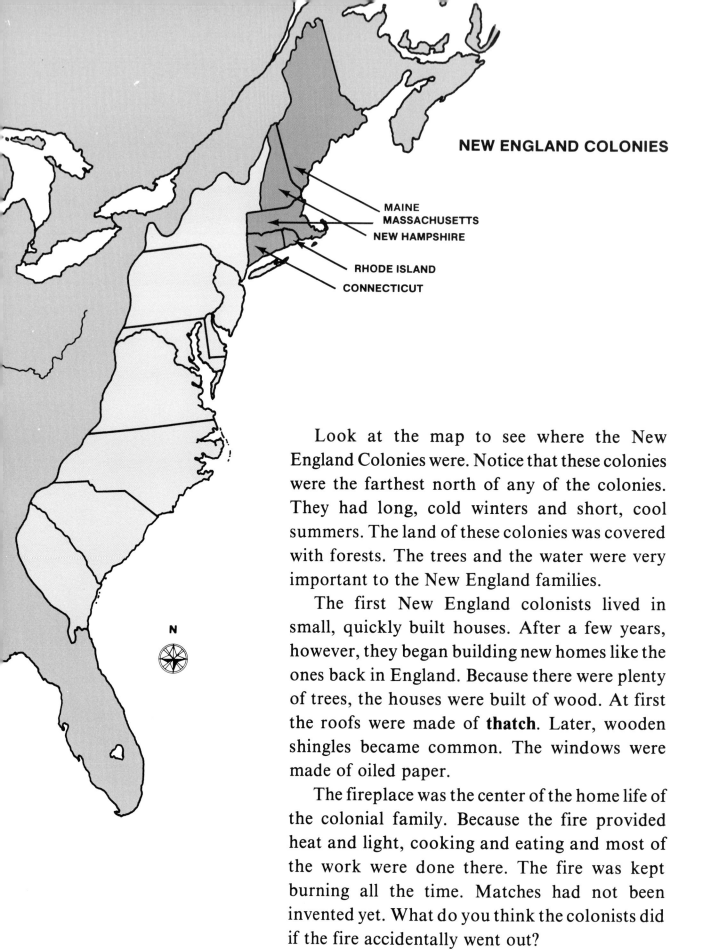

**NEW ENGLAND COLONIES**

MAINE
MASSACHUSETTS
NEW HAMPSHIRE
RHODE ISLAND
CONNECTICUT

N

Look at the map to see where the New England Colonies were. Notice that these colonies were the farthest north of any of the colonies. They had long, cold winters and short, cool summers. The land of these colonies was covered with forests. The trees and the water were very important to the New England families.

The first New England colonists lived in small, quickly built houses. After a few years, however, they began building new homes like the ones back in England. Because there were plenty of trees, the houses were built of wood. At first the roofs were made of **thatch**. Later, wooden shingles became common. The windows were made of oiled paper.

The fireplace was the center of the home life of the colonial family. Because the fire provided heat and light, cooking and eating and most of the work were done there. The fire was kept burning all the time. Matches had not been invented yet. What do you think the colonists did if the fire accidentally went out?

The bedrooms of these houses were very cold in winter, because they were not heated. Beds were made of mattresses placed on the floor or on a net of woven ropes. The mattresses were stuffed with cornhusks, straw, or feathers. Curtains were often hung around the beds to help keep out cold air. Quilts and feather coverlets kept the sleepers warm.

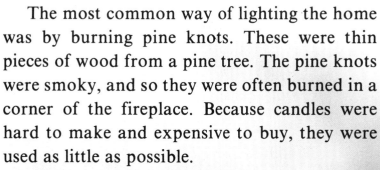

The most common way of lighting the home was by burning pine knots. These were thin pieces of wood from a pine tree. The pine knots were smoky, and so they were often burned in a corner of the fireplace. Because candles were hard to make and expensive to buy, they were used as little as possible.

The first lamps were called Betty lamps. They were filled with fish oil or whale oil or with grease from cooking. A wick was laid in the lamp so that the end hung out the spout. The wick burned with a smoky, dull, bad-smelling flame.

Fish for breakfast! Fish for dinner! Fish for supper! The streams, rivers, and oceans were full of fish. Nearly everyone ate fish every day. Codfish were especially plentiful. Great lobsters were easy to catch. Salmon was so common that it cost less than one cent a pound.

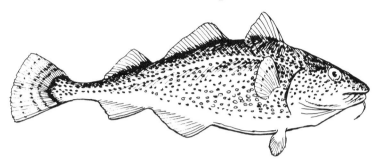

Farms in New England were small. The soil was full of stones. The summers were short and cool. The crops that grew best were corn, beans, squash, and pumpkins. The Indians taught the colonists how to plant them.

First, the soil was loosened and made into small hills. A little fish was buried in the soil for fertilizer. A few kernels of corn were put into each hill. Beans were planted in the same hill so that the beans could climb on the stalks of corn. Squash and pumpkins were planted between the hills.

During the first two years of the Plymouth colony, the settlers planted their field together. Everyone did part of the work, and everyone shared the crop. This way of farming did not work. Some men did not work hard but wanted a full share of the harvest.

Starting with the third year, each farmer had his own field in which to grow his own crop. This was a better way. The families worked harder when they knew they could have all of what they grew.

*Boston, Massachusetts*

It was March 1630. Eleven ships sailed from England for America. Seven hundred passengers came on seven of the ships. The other four ships were loaded with farm animals and supplies. The leader of these colonists was a wealthy man named John Winthrop.

These people had two reasons for leaving England. First, they wanted freedom to worship God in their own way. Second, they wanted to have a chance to earn money and have a comfortable home. These colonists were called **Puritans**.

The ships arrived in Massachusetts in June. The colonists came in time to plant their crops. In a few weeks they started to build their first town on a peninsula in the bay. They called their town Boston.

At first, everything went quite well. Then winter came. About two hundred persons died from sickness. A fire broke out and burned several buildings. When a ship from England came in February, eighty settlers decided to go back on it. Governor Winthrop encouraged the remaining colonists to trust God to supply their needs. He told them they must not quit.

The next summer hundreds of Puritans came from England to join those in America. They brought saws, kettles, guns, window glass, cloth, and many other supplies that were needed. Among these people were carpenters, millers, tanners, shoemakers, and tailors. Homes were built, businesses were started, and the town of Boston began to grow.

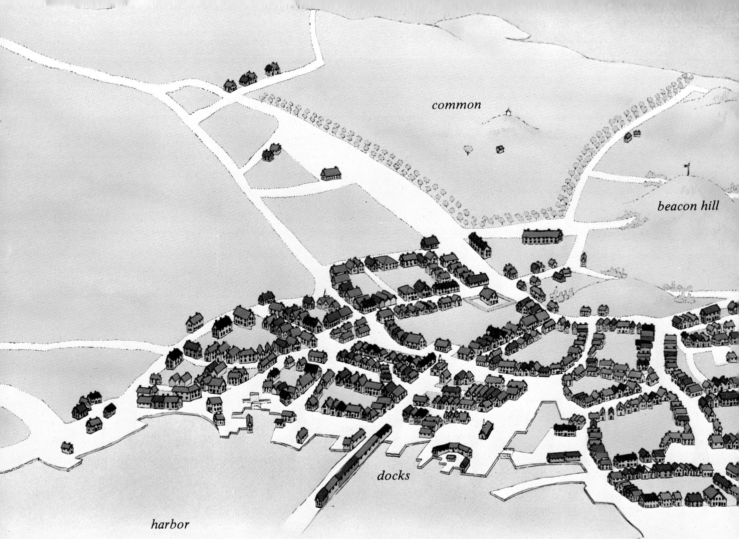

common

beacon hill

harbor

docks

Find the **Common** on the map. This piece of land was a pastureland. Each family that lived in the town was allowed to pasture one or two cows or as many as five goats in this field. Each morning from spring until fall, a cowherd would go through the town to get the animals. He would drive them to the Common to graze. At six o'clock in the evening he would bring them back to their owners.

Several years passed. Boston needed work for the many persons who were coming there. Governor Winthrop and other men started ship-building businesses. The bay and ocean were full of fish, so many men went into the fishing business. Thousands of barrels of dried codfish were shipped to England and other countries to be sold. Soon Boston was a large, important town.

Spinning and weaving were important in the New England Colonies. Each family made wool and linen cloth. They made the cloth for their own clothing and also to trade for goods that they could not make for themselves.

A spinning wheel stood in every home. Everyone in the family, even the children, had a part in making cloth.

Families were encouraged to raise sheep. The sheep were permitted to graze in the commons. No sheep under two years old could be killed for food. If a dog killed a sheep, the dog's owner had to hang the dog and pay the sheep's owner double the cost of the sheep.

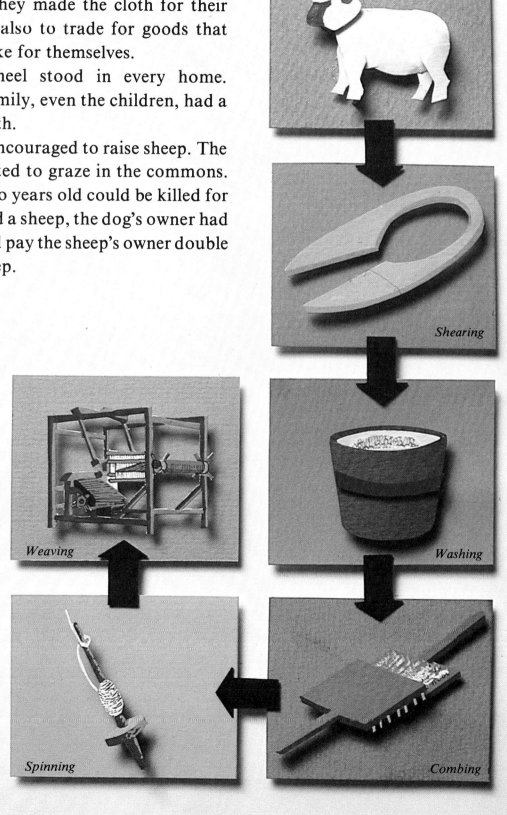

*Shearing*

*Weaving*

*Washing*

*Spinning*

*Combing*

The settlers ate corn, also called maize, every day. During the summer they boiled some on the cob much as we do today. They also cut some off the cob and then boiled it. The Indians called this **succotash**. Most of the corn was allowed to ripen. Then it was shelled and ground into cornmeal. The meal was made into "hasty pudding," "johnnycake," or "rye-an'-injun" bread.

Boys usually shelled the corn. Every evening all winter long, they sat by the fireplace and scraped the ears of corn on the edge of a shovel or some other sharp object. This removed the kernels from the cob.

At first the women ground the corn by hand as the Indians did. Soon, mills were built. Some mills were run by the wind, but most of them were water mills. The miller was usually given one-sixth of the meal to pay him for his work.

Governor Winthrop of the Massachusetts colony wrote about a kind of corn that turned inside out when it was "parched" and that was "white and floury within." What kind of corn do you think he was talking about?

The pumpkin was an important food for the early colonists. It was easy to grow, easy to cook, and easy to store. One colonial poet wrote, "We have pumpkins at morning and pumpkins at noon. If it were not for pumpkins, we should be undone."

The settlers brought trees, plants, and seeds of many kinds to America. In a few years they were able to enjoy apples, pears, plums, and many other foods that we have today. They also brought cows and sheep so that they would have milk to drink and meat to eat. The men also hunted deer and other animals to provide meat.

Most families did not have white sugar. They sweetened their food with honey or maple sugar. Where do you think they got these?

Can you imagine eating without a fork? The first fork brought to America was for Governor Winthrop. Forks were not in common use for about a hundred years after that. Everyone ate with just a spoon and a knife.

The early colonists did not have plates or bowls either. Instead, they set their tables with **trenchers**. A trencher was a block of wood that was hollowed into a sort of bowl. Two people shared one trencher.

Cups and mugs were made of horn, wood, **pewter**, or even gourds. Wealthy people often brought silver cups from England. Usually everyone in the family drank from the same cup.

Many times children did not sit at the table with the adults. They stood by the table at their places. They were not allowed to speak unless they were spoken to. They were not allowed to ask for anything on the table.

Each member of the colonial family had responsibilities. The father was the head of the home. He had to make sure that his wife and children had a place to live, food to eat, and clothes to wear. The Christian father taught his family about God, the need to be saved, and the importance of living in a way that would please God. The mother's responsibility was to care for the house and the children. The children's responsibility was to help the parents in every way they could and to learn to be a good adult.

Are the responsibilities of the members of your family different from those of the colonial family?

83

The New England colonists held church services every Sunday. If they had no church building, they met outside under a tree, in a fort, in someone's house, or in some other building. When they built a church building, it was usually in the center of the town. It was often called the **meeting house.**

The beginning of a church service was announced by the blowing of a great **conch** shell or a trumpet or by the beating of a drum. Men and women sat on opposite sides of the building. Little girls sat with their mothers, and the boys sat together. One town ordered that "all ye boyes of ye towne are appointed to sitt upon ye three paire of stairs in ye meeting house, and Wm. Lord is appointed to look after ye boyes upon ye pulpit stairs."

The churches were very uncomfortable in the winter because they were not heated. Some churches had wolfskin bags nailed to the seats so that the people could put their legs into them. Dogs were allowed to lie on their masters' feet to help keep them warm. Most women carried foot stoves. These were little metal boxes that held hot coals. The women put their feet on top of the stoves. Even with these things, the people were still very cold.

The church services were long. There was always a prayer and a sermon in each service. Each of these might be two hours long. Sometimes it took half an hour to sing one psalm. There were very few psalmbooks and these had no notes. A deacon would read a line, and then the congregation would sing that line. Then he would read another line, and the people would sing it. This went on until the psalm ended. There were no pianos or organs. The people knew about eight tunes, and these were used over and over for the different psalms.

The colonists had many laws concerning the way Sunday could be spent. No one was allowed to work, hunt, fish, or play from sunset on Saturday until sunset on Sunday. Anyone who disobeyed these laws had to pay a fine or be punished in some other way.

## PSALME xCix, C.

and he *alone*
   them anſwer gave.
7 He unto them did ſpeake
   it'h cloudy pillar: *then*
they kept his records, eke
his ord'nance he gave them.
8   Lord, thou who art
our God didſt heare,
  & didſt anſwer
   to them impart,
Thou waſt a God pard'ning
them, although thou vengeance
upon their works didſt bring.
9  The Lord our God advance,
  & bow yee downe
at's holy hill:
for our God's *ſtil*
  the Holy-one.
    Pſalme 100.
   A *Pſalme of prayſe.*

Make yee a joyfull ſounding noyſe unto Iehovah, all the earth:
2 Serve yee Iehovah with gladnes:
before his preſence come with mirth.
3  Know, that Iehovah he is God,
who hath us formed it is hee,
& not our ſelves: his owne people
& ſheepe of his paſture are wee.
4  Enter into his gates with prayſe,
into his Courts with thankfullnes:
make yee confeſſion unto him,

## PSALM C, Cr.

& his name reverently bleſſe.
5   Becauſe Iehovah he is good,
for evermore is his mercy:
& unto generations all
continue doth his verity.
   *Another of the ſame.*

Make yee a joyfull noyſe unto Iehovah all the earth:
2 Serve yee Iehovah with gladnes:
  before him come with mirth.
3 Know, that Iehovah he is God,
  not wee our ſelves, but hee
hath made us: his people, & ſheep
of his paſture are wee.
4  O enter yee into his gates
  with prayſe, & thankfullneſſe
into his Courts: confeſſe to him,
  & his Name doe yee bleſſe.
5 Becauſe Iehovah he is good,
  his bounteous-mercy
is everlaſting: & his truth
  is to eternity.
    Pſalme 101.
   A pſalme of David.

Mercy & judgement I will ſing, Lord, I will ſing to thee.
2 I'le wiſely doe in perfect way:
  when wilt thou come to mee?
I will in midſt of my houſe walk
  in my hearts perfectnes:
3 I will not ſet before mine eyes

In *Adam's* Fall
We Sinned all.

Thy Life to Mend
This *Book* Attend.

*Job* feels the Rod
Yet blesses GOD.

*Whales* in the Sea
God's Voice obey.

*Xerxes* the great did
die,
And so must you & I.

*Rhymes from the* New England Primer

The colonists in New England knew that it was important that children learn to read. (A person cannot read the Bible if he does not know how to read, and a Christian should read the Bible each day.) Children between the ages of five and eight usually went to a **dame school**. This kind of school was held in a home, and the teacher was the woman of the home.

The children often learned from a **hornbook**. A hornbook was a board with a sheet of paper fastened to it. The alphabet, numerals, and perhaps the Lord's Prayer were written on the paper. A thin, clear piece of horn covered the paper.

When the villages grew large enough, other schools were started. Only boys attended these schools. The Bible, a catechism, a psalmbook, and the *New England Primer* were the only books in many schools.

———◆———

### THE TEN COMMANDMENTS,

PUT INTO SHORT AND EASY RHYMES FOR
CHILDREN.

1. Thou shalt have no more gods but me.
2. Before no idol bend thy knee.
3. Take not the name of God in vain.
4. Dare not the Sabbath day profane.
5. Give both thy parents honor due.
6. Take heed that thou no murder do.
7. Abstain from words and deeds unclean.
8. Steal not, though thou be poor and mean.
9. Make not a wilful lie, nor love it.
10. What is thy neighbor's, dare not covet.

The children in the New England Colonies helped their parents most of each day, but they had some time to play. They liked to run races, ice-skate, and play games such as tag and blindman's buff. The boys played a game something like our football. The girls liked to play house. Their dolls were sometimes made of cornhusks.

Life in the New England Colonies was not easy. The homes were not comfortable, and the work was hard, but the people did not return to England. They stayed in America where they had freedom to worship God as they pleased.

*Obedience to God*

"Then Peter and the other apostles answered and said, We ought to obey God rather than men."

Acts 5:29

## New words

colonists

colony

common

conch

dame school

hornbook

Mayflower Compact

meeting house

pewter

pilgrim

Puritan

scurvy

settlers

succotash

thatch

trencher

## Things to remember

Read each sentence. Choose the correct answer needed to fill in each blank.

1. The New England winters are _____. (short and cold, long and cold, long and cool, short and cool)

2. The soil in New England is _____. (rich and sandy, poor and stony)

3. Most of the houses in New England were made of _____. (wood, brick, stone)

4. Many New England colonists ate their meals from _____. (china plates, glass bowls, wooden trenchers)

5. The open fields where animals grazed were called _____. (plains, commons, yards)

6. Two important foods in early New England were _____. (corn and potatoes, corn and pumpkins, corn and tomatoes)

7. The alphabet with short rhymed verses was found in the _____. (*New England Primer,* hornbook, psalmbook)

8. Maize was the Indian name for _____. (squash, beans, corn)

## Things to talk about

1. What are some ways your school is different from schools in the New England colonies?

2. What are some ways your church is different from New England churches?

3. Why is it important for Christians to know how to read?

4. What responsibilities did colonial boys and girls have that boys and girls today do not have?

5. What do you have in your home that makes it more comfortable than a colonial home?

6. What are some ways that Indian families, colonial families, and your family are alike?

7. What are some natural resources of New England? How did the colonists use them?

8. What do we mean by freedom of religion?

## Things to do

1. Put the names of the New England colonies on a map that your teacher gives you. Color them light blue.

2. Get a pumpkin. Bake and salt the seeds. Make a pie from the "flesh."

3. Make some johnnycakes. Eat them with honey.

4. Make a hornbook.

5. Shell and grind some corn.

6. Sing a psalm that your teacher "lines out" to you.

7. Find the cost of salmon.

8. Find a recipe for succotash. What is in it besides corn?

9. Make a doll from cornhusks.

10. List the ways you have eaten corn.

11. Find out how maple sugar is produced.

# 5 The Middle Colonies

## Goals

1. I will be able to locate the Middle Colonies on a map of North America.
2. I will be able to describe the land of the Middle Colonies.
3. I will be able to tell the reason that the Middle Colonies were called the "bread colonies."
4. I will be able to explain how candles and soap were made.
5. I will be able to tell something the Dutch and Swedish colonists added to our heritage.
6. I will work "heartily, as to the Lord."

The first colonists in the Middle Colonies were not English. Many of them were Dutch and Swedish. Most did not come to America to worship God. They came so that they could own their own land. Later, great numbers of English and German people came to these colonies. Soon there was a mixture of languages, customs, and ideas. But all of these people were Americans.

### New York, New York

In 1625 a small group of Dutch colonists started a settlement on an island we call Manhattan. They brought two shiploads of horses, cattle, sheep, hogs, seeds, and plows with them. They called their settlement New Amsterdam.

The next year Peter Minuit came to the little village to be their leader. One of the first things he did was to buy the island of Manhattan from the Indians. He paid them with beads and ribbons worth about twenty-four dollars.

The village of New Amsterdam grew slowly. The people made their living by farming and by trading with the Indians for furs. The furs were sent to Europe to be sold.

Later Peter Stuyvesant came to New Amsterdam to be the governor of the Dutch colony. He had lost a leg in a war and was sometimes called "Old Silver Leg."

Peter tried to be a good leader. He made laws saying that people must build fences so that their cows, sheep, and pigs could not wander through the streets. He also made a law forbidding people to throw their garbage into the streets. He directed men in building a dock into deep water so that ships could load and unload easily. Governor Stuyvesant worked out a way to fight fires. When a building caught on fire, everyone had to help carry buckets of water to put the fire out.

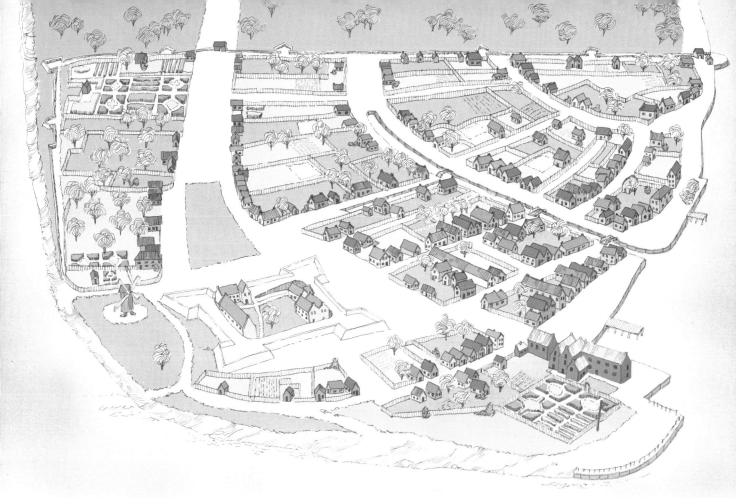

Many people were not happy in this Dutch colony. The people did not have a part in making the laws, and they had to pay high taxes.

In 1664 some English ships sailed into the harbor near New Amsterdam. A letter was given to Peter Stuyvesant asking that the colony surrender to England. The letter promised that the people could keep their homes and keep on with the kind of work they were already doing. The Dutch governor was so angry that he tore the letter into pieces.

Three of his friends gathered the pieces and put them back together. They read the letter to the townspeople. The townspeople decided that they would rather be ruled by the English than by the Dutch. They raised a white flag over their fort. Then the colony belonged to England. The English changed the name from New Amsterdam to New York.

In 1638 Peter Minuit returned to America. This time he was the leader of a small group of people from Sweden. These colonists built a fort and named it *Christiana* after their queen. They called their colony New Sweden.

After a few years New Sweden was taken over by the Dutch. Still later it became a part of the English colony called Delaware.

The Swedish people built homes like the ones they had had in Sweden. These were small cabins built from logs.

Log cabins were good homes for the colonists. The land was covered with forests that had to be cut. Only a few tools were needed to prepare the logs. A cabin could be put up in a short time.

Seventy or eighty trees were needed to build a cabin. The logs had to be about the same size. Usually they were about ten inches thick. Notches were cut near the ends of the logs so that they would fit together at the corners.

The logs were used in pairs. Two logs were put on the sides, and then two were put on the ends. When the walls were about seven feet high, extra logs were sometimes used to make a floor for a loft. Next, the roof was made. It was covered with bark or thin pieces of wood cut from trees. The cracks between the logs were filled with moss, clay, or a mixture of these.

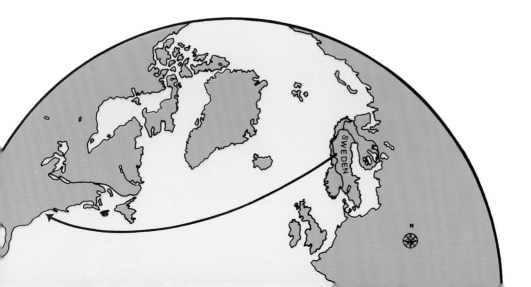

An opening was made for a door, which was hung with leather hinges. Some cabins had windows. These were covered with animal skins or wooden shutters. Usually another opening was made for a fireplace.

Most of the Swedish settlers had a second log house that they used for a bathhouse. This little house had a fireplace in one corner where stones were heated. Water was poured over the hot stones. This made steam. The person taking a bath sat in the steam for a while. Then he ran outside and jumped into the river or rolled in the snow. Today we call a place where a person can take a steam bath a **sauna**.

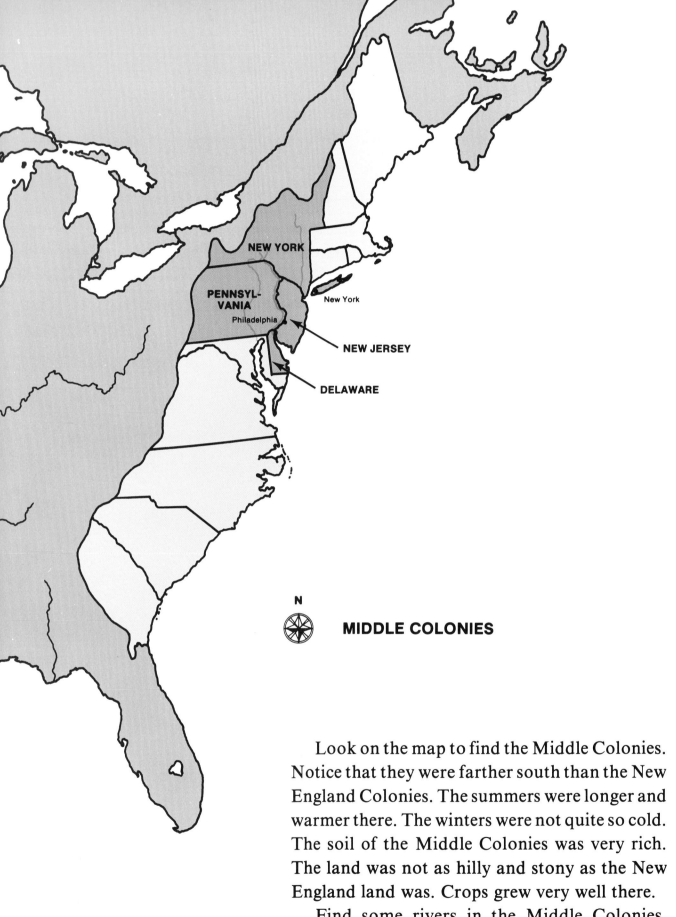

NEW YORK

PENNSYL-
VANIA

Philadelphia

New York

NEW JERSEY

DELAWARE

N

MIDDLE COLONIES

Look on the map to find the Middle Colonies. Notice that they were farther south than the New England Colonies. The summers were longer and warmer there. The winters were not quite so cold. The soil of the Middle Colonies was very rich. The land was not as hilly and stony as the New England land was. Crops grew very well there.

Find some rivers in the Middle Colonies. Notice where the cities were located.

The Dutch often made their houses partly of stone or brick. The windows were covered with shutters. The door was usually made in two parts. The top half could be opened while the bottom half stayed closed.

These homes had one main room where the great fireplace was built. There were small rooms on the sides. Each home had a **garret** and a cellar.

Many of these homes had parlors. A parlor was a very special room. It was thoroughly cleaned every week. The floors were scrubbed, the windows were washed, and the furniture was polished. Then the door was locked, and no one could go in. This room was used only for very important visitors.

Nearly everyone slept on mattresses stuffed with goose feathers. They used coverlets filled with goose **down**. You can understand why each family kept a flock of geese. Twice a year each goose would be caught and most of its small feathers and down would be pulled out. A stocking would be pulled over the goose's head to keep it from biting while it was being plucked. When a goose was killed to be eaten, all the feathers were saved. The long stiff feathers were called **quills.** People would write with them.

These colonists used dishes made of pottery and pewter as well as wood. Many of them brought silver mugs and bowls from their old homes in Europe. They kept their dishes on open shelves in the kitchen.

Food in the Middle Colonies was plentiful. The farmers raised fine cows, and so they had milk, butter, and cheese. Since they raised pigs, they had ham, bacon, and sausage. Deer were so common that they were often seen in the barnyards eating with the farm animals. There were many wild turkeys in the forests. The river and bays were full of fish.

Since the colonists grew wheat, they were able to have white bread as well as cornbread. They sold so much wheat and wheat flour that they were known as the "bread colonies."

The early colonists ate most of the vegetables that we eat today, but they did not have potatoes or tomatoes. The Dutch often ate a salad made of sliced cabbage. They called it **koolslaa**. We call it coleslaw.

The colonists brought fruit trees to America and planted great orchards. Apples, peaches, and plums were so plentiful that they could not all be eaten. Apples were especially popular. They were eaten as applesauce or apple butter and in apple pies and tarts.

A man living in Delaware wrote the following description of colonial apple pie:

> Apple pie is used throughout the whole year, and when fresh apples are no longer to be had, dried ones are used. It is the evening meal of children. House pie, in country places, is made of apples neither peeled nor freed from their cores, and its crust is not broken if a wagon wheel goes over it.

The cellar was used to store food for winter. There were great bins of apples, parsnips, and turnips. Strong barrels of vinegar and cider lay on great racks. Kegs of corned beef, salt pork, salted fish, and butter stood on the floor. Jars of pickles and spiced fruit lined the shelves.

Every autumn the colonial women made soap. It was made from grease and lye. Grease from cooking was saved all year long. Lye was made by pouring water into a barrel filled with ashes. A small hole was put near the bottom of the barrel and the lye trickled out through the hole into a kettle. The grease and lye were boiled together in a large pot over a fire out of doors. It was carefully stirred while it cooked. The German women always stirred with a **sassafras** stick. When the soap was finished, it looked like soft clear jelly. A good worker could make a barrel of soap in one day. This soft soap was the only kind of soap most families used.

How often does your mother do laundry? Most colonial women washed clothes and bedding only once a month.

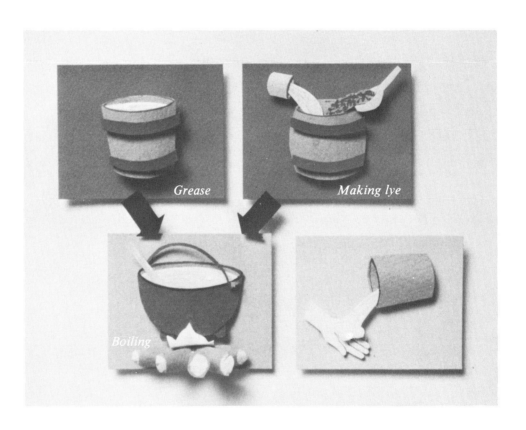

Grease

Making lye

Boiling

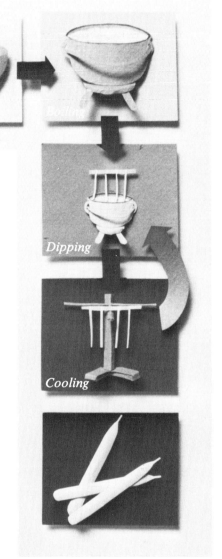

Another responsibility of the colonial housewife was making candles. Tallow candles were made from the fat of cattle, deer, moose, or bears. Wax candles were made from honeycomb or from bayberries.

Bayberry bushes grew near the coast in all the colonies. Ripe berries were gathered and put in large pots with boiling water. The wax in the berries melted and floated to the top of the water. The clear green wax hardened when it cooled. Candles made from this wax burned well and had a good smell. It took about four quarts of bayberries to make one candle.

Some candles were made by dipping. Several wicks were fastened to a candle rod. The wicks were dipped into a kettle of hot wax or tallow and then set aside to cool. This was done again and again until the candles were thick enough. A good worker could make two hundred candles in one day.

Candles were also made by pouring wax or tallow into molds.

Can you guess how many candles were needed by a family for one year? If a house had five rooms and one candle was burned in each room each night, 1,825 candles would be burned in a year. Do you think this would be enough?

The children of the Dutch colonists who settled New York eagerly waited for December 6. This was called Saint Nicholas Day. Saint Nicholas was supposed to have been a good man who came back to earth on that day each year to give gifts to good children and birch rods to bad children. Sometimes Saint Nicholas was called "Sinterklass."

As years went by, "Sinterklass" became Santa Claus. The saint's red robe became a fur-trimmed suit. His white horse was replaced by eight tiny reindeer. His home was changed from heaven to the North Pole.

There were schools in the Middle Colonies, but many of them were not very good. One problem was that many of the students spoke Dutch or German at home, and the teacher taught in English.

One teacher used this plan to make his students speak English. Each day he gave a metal button to the first person who used a Dutch word. That person could give it to another student whom he heard speaking Dutch. The button was passed from person to person throughout the day. The boy who had the button at the end of the day was spanked.

If you were a colonial girl in a Dutch or German family, you probably would not go to school. Your parents might teach you at home to read in your language. You probably would not learn to write at all. You would be taught to cook, spin, sew, knit, and do the other things necessary to keeping house. Many girls were able to knit their own stockings by the time they were five years old.

Almost every girl made a sampler. This is one
made by a girl named Janet Whitehouse.

The children in the Middle Colonies loved to play. Like children today, they played tag and ran races. They also played a game called "whoop and hide," which was like hide-and-seek. Their favorite toys were tops, marbles, and dolls.

In summer they played croquet and ninepins. Ninepins is something like bowling, but it is played outside on a level, grassy place.

Winter sports were the most fun of all. Both adults and children enjoyed ice-skating and coasting on sleds.

Sunday was a day of rest. People were not required to go to church, but they had to be quiet during the time of a service. Working, hunting, fishing, and playing in the streets were not allowed. Often people who disobeyed the Sunday laws were put in **stocks**. A cage was built in the center of some towns. Boys who broke the Sunday laws were punished by being put into it.

The services in some churches were in Dutch or German because many people could not read an English Bible or psalmbook. The sermons and prayers were shorter than those in the New England churches. The parents did not always take the babies and small children to church.

The offering was collected in a velvet bag on the end of a long pole. A small bell was fastened to the bag. It would ring when a coin was dropped in.

*Philadelphia, Pennsylvania*

William Penn wanted to try an experiment. He called it "an holy experiment." He decided to start a colony in America where every person could worship God as he pleased even if it was different from the way the leaders worshiped. But he needed a place to try the experiment.

The king of England owed the Penn family a large amount of money. Instead of paying the debt with money, he gave William a large piece of land in America. William called the land "Sylvania," which means "woods." The king called it Pennsylvania or "Penn's Woods." Now the experiment could begin.

*William Penn making an
agreement with the Indians*

The good news about William Penn's colony spread rapidly. All religions would be free. A farm could be bought for about fifty dollars. The people would make the laws. The land was rich and crops would grow well.

More than twenty ships carrying about three thousand passengers sailed to Pennsylvania. Many of these colonists were from England. People of different religions came from Germany, Holland, and Northern Ireland.

William Penn and his family arrived in Pennsylvania in 1682. One day he saw a level place where two rivers met. He decided that it was just right for a city he had planned.

The city was laid out like a checkerboard. The streets that went toward the rivers were named after trees that grew there. Some streets were Walnut Street, Chestnut Street, Spruce Street, and Cedar Street. All the streets that crossed these streets were numbered, except the street that ran along the river front. It was named Front Street. The other streets were Second Street, Third Street, and so on. This city was called Philadelphia. Philadelphia means "the city of brotherly love."

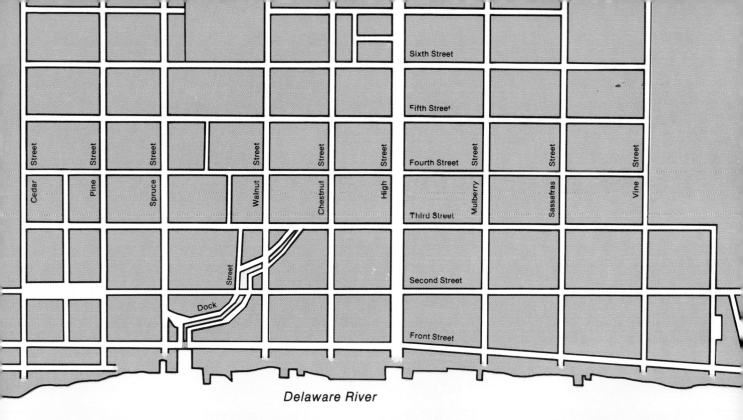

Sixth Street

Fifth Street

Fourth Street

Third Street

Second Street

Front Street

Cedar Street

Pine Street

Spruce Street

Walnut Street

Chestnut Street

High Street

Mulberry Street

Sassafras Street

Vine Street

Dock Street

*Delaware River*

## PHILADELPHIA

NORTH →

Philadelphia grew rapidly. In just two years 357 houses were built. Many of these were made of bright red brick. Men and women started businesses. There were shopkeepers, tailors, candlemakers, printers, seamstresses, and **apothecaries**. By 1750 Philadelphia was the largest city in the American colonies.

Life in the Middle Colonies was not so hard as in the New England Colonies. The farmers worked hard and produced more crops than they could use. They could sell or trade the extra and be able to build better houses. They could make their homes more comfortable and have nicer clothes. This gave more jobs to carpenters, candlemakers, blacksmiths, tailors, and other workers.

Some settlers came to the Middle Colonies to have freedom of religion. More settlers came so that they could own their own farm or business. They all wanted to have the good things of life for themselves and for their families.

*Eagerness to Work*

"And whatsoever ye do, do it heartily, as to the Lord, and not unto men."

Colossians 3:23

## New words

apothecary

down

garret

koolslaa

quill

sassafras

sauna

stocks

## Things to remember

Read each sentence. Choose the correct answer needed to fill in each blank.

1. Long, stiff feathers are called _____. (squills, quills, quilts)
2. Ham and bacon are made from the meat of _____. (pigs, cows, chickens)
3. Coleslaw is made from _____. (spinach, lettuce, cabbage)
4. White bread is usually made from _____. (wheat flour, rye flour, cornmeal)
5. The early colonists did not eat _____. (turnips, tomatoes, peaches)
6. Bayberries were used to make _____. (soap, candles, pie)
7. A sampler is made by _____. (cooking, spinning, sewing)

## Things to talk about

1. Why do you think the teachers in the schools of the Middle Colonies wanted everyone to speak English?
2. Why do you think the offering bag at church had a bell on it? Do you think this was a good idea? Why?
3. What games do you play that the children of the Middle Colonies played?

4. Does your house have a parlor? Is it used like the colonists used theirs?

5. How is "house pie" as described in the unit different from the apple pie we eat today?

6. Why do you think the colonists believed that girls did not need to learn to write?

7. What does the message on the sampler on page 103 mean?

8. Is the service in your church more like the services in the Middle Colonies or the New England Colonies?

9. Name some ways the Middle Colonies were different from the New England Colonies.

10. Why is Santa Claus sometimes called Saint Nick?

## Things to do

1. Put the names of the Middle Colonies on your map. Color them yellow.

2. Make a candle by dipping a wick into wax or tallow. Make a candle by filling a mold with wax.

3. Smell a bayberry candle.

4. Light a room at night with just one candle. See if the room is light enough so that you can see to read.

5. Make apple butter.

6. Find how other Christmas customs began.

7. Tell how your family celebrates Christmas and other special days.

8. Try to write with a quill. (You will need some ink.)

9. Taste some dried apples.

10. Make a sampler.

# 6 The Southern Colonies

# Goals

1 I will be able to locate the Southern Colonies on a map of North America.

2 I will be able to describe the land of the Southern Colonies.

3 I will be able to list the main crops of the Southern Colonies.

4 I will be able to describe life on a large plantation.

5 I will be able to explain where the names of some people and places came from.

6 I will praise the Lord each day.

The first English colony in America was Virginia. Many of the leaders of this southern colony were from rich families. They were interested in making money and having fine homes.

The last of the thirteen colonies started in America was Georgia. Many of its people were poor, and most of them were in debt.

Today our country is made up of different kinds of people, just as it was then. God loves us all. He wants everyone to become a Christian and to live for Him.

*Jamestown, Virginia*

One spring day in 1607 three English ships sailed up a river near the east coast of America. One hundred four men had come on these ships to start a settlement in Virginia. They picked a peninsula about sixty miles up the river for a place to build. They called their settlement Jamestown after King James of England.

Captain John Smith was one of the most important leaders of the English settlers. He directed the men as they built rough houses and a church. This is how he described their first church.

"Wee did hang an awning, which is an old saile, to three or foure trees to shadow us from the Sunne; our walls were railes of wood; our seats unhewed trees till we cut planks; our Pulput a bar of wood nailed to two neighboring trees."

*wattle and daub house*

113

The English settlers did not know how to live in the new land. Many wanted to look for gold and silver instead of planting crops. Captain Smith was a good leader. He did what he thought was right even when it made him unpopular. He told the men that if they would not work, they could not eat. But soon the settlers had little food. Many became sick and died. By autumn only thirty-eight men remained.

The settlers often saw Indians. They called them "redskins" because the Indians painted their bodies red. Captain Smith learned to trade with the Indians. He got corn and other kinds of food from them.

The Indian chief's daughter, Pocahontas, became a good friend of the white men. She often brought them food. She helped keep peace between the English and the Indians.

As the years passed, more colonists came to Jamestown. Many brought their families, but still Jamestown was a small settlement.

One day Captain Smith was injured when some gunpowder exploded. He decided to return to England.

Now the colony was in trouble. They did not have a good leader. Besides, they did not have good businesses so that they could earn money. The settlers knew that they must find a product to sell in England or they would fail.

John Rolfe was a young man in Jamestown. He decided to plant tobacco. He knew that early English explorers had taken samples of tobacco back to England after they had found the Indians smoking it in America. King James said that smoking was "lothsome to the eye, hatefull to the nose, harmfull to the braine, dangerous to the lungs," but many men smoked it anyway.

Mr. Rolfe sent a large amount of tobacco to England. It sold for a good price. Soon nearly every Jamestown family grew tobacco. Now the settlement of Jamestown began to grow.

John Rolfe married an Indian girl named Pocahontas. It may have been the same girl that had helped the settlers years before.

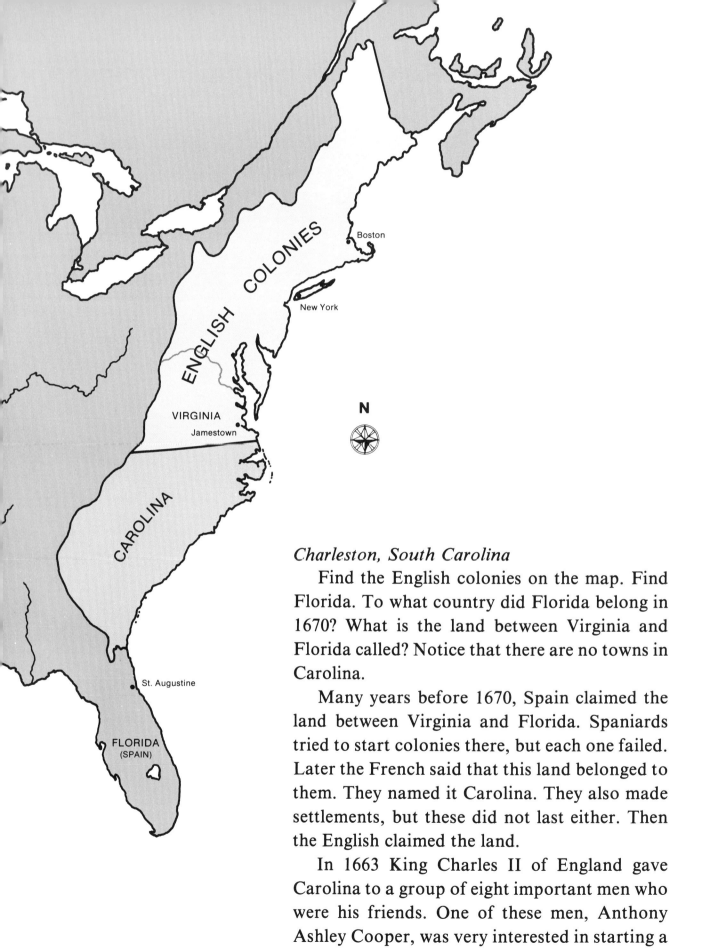

*Charleston, South Carolina*

Find the English colonies on the map. Find Florida. To what country did Florida belong in 1670? What is the land between Virginia and Florida called? Notice that there are no towns in Carolina.

Many years before 1670, Spain claimed the land between Virginia and Florida. Spaniards tried to start colonies there, but each one failed. Later the French said that this land belonged to them. They named it Carolina. They also made settlements, but these did not last either. Then the English claimed the land.

In 1663 King Charles II of England gave Carolina to a group of eight important men who were his friends. One of these men, Anthony Ashley Cooper, was very interested in starting a colony in the new world. He thought that it would be good for England. Besides, he hoped that he would make money from it for himself.

While plans for the colony were being made, Captain William Hilton was sent on a voyage to explore the coast of Carolina. He and his men found a rich land with tall oak and pine trees. He saw that the Indians grew corn, pumpkins, watermelons, and muskmelons. He saw great amounts of grapes, figs, and peaches. Captain Hilton reported that most of the Indians were friendly.

In April 1670, about 130 persons reached Carolina on a ship called the *Carolina*. They decided to build their first houses on a point of land a few miles from the ocean. What did they name the rivers that met at that point?

The colonists had not brought a large supply of food with them, but they did not go hungry. They traded with the Indians for food. They hunted and fished. Soon they sent a boat to Virginia to bring back cattle and pigs.

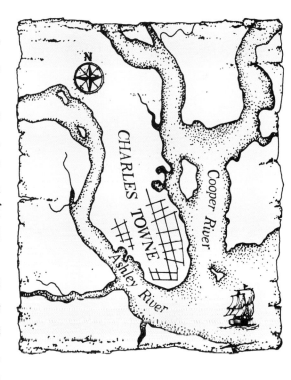

The colonists realized that they were in some danger from the Spanish and unfriendly Indians, so they built a wall around their town. They also set up seven great guns for protection. The town was named Charles Towne after the king of England. Many years later the name was changed to Charleston.

Settlers from Europe came to live in Charles Towne. A group of Christians from France came because they did not have freedom to obey the Bible in their homeland. Families from Holland, Scotland, and Ireland came to start a new life in America. The colony grew.

Troubles came to Charles Towne. Once a fire burned almost half of the town. Later a hurricane struck and destroyed many buildings. But the people rebuilt the town. Even when diseases spread and killed many people, some of the people did not leave their homes.

In 1694 a storm drove a ship into the Charles Towne harbor. It was carrying a load of rice. The captain gave a bag of seed to a farmer. The rice grew so well that other farmers decided to grow it too. Soon ships from many countries came to Charles Towne to buy rice. Many families became rich.

If you visit Charleston today, you can see homes that were built almost 200 years ago. You can see beautiful gardens and parks. The people of Charleston are proud of their heritage.

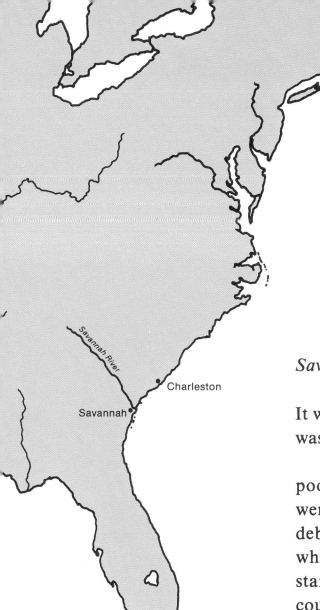

*John Wesley*

## Savannah, Georgia

Georgia was the last of the thirteen colonies. It was started in 1732. Its most important leader was James Oglethorpe.

Mr. Oglethorpe was concerned about the poor people in England. He knew that many men were put in jail because they could not pay their debts. One of his friends had died of smallpox while he was in jail. James Oglethorpe wanted to start a colony in America where poor people could go to start a new life.

King George II of England gave him permission to start a colony on the land between Florida and South Carolina. James Oglethorpe and his colonists from England built Fort Savannah near the Savannah River. There were no important crops or businesses in Georgia, and the colony grew very slowly.

Two famous preachers from England spent time in Georgia. John Wesley came to be a missionary. He started the first Sunday school in America. Mr. Wesley returned to England after a short time. George Whitefield preached in America for many years. He started an orphanage in Savannah.

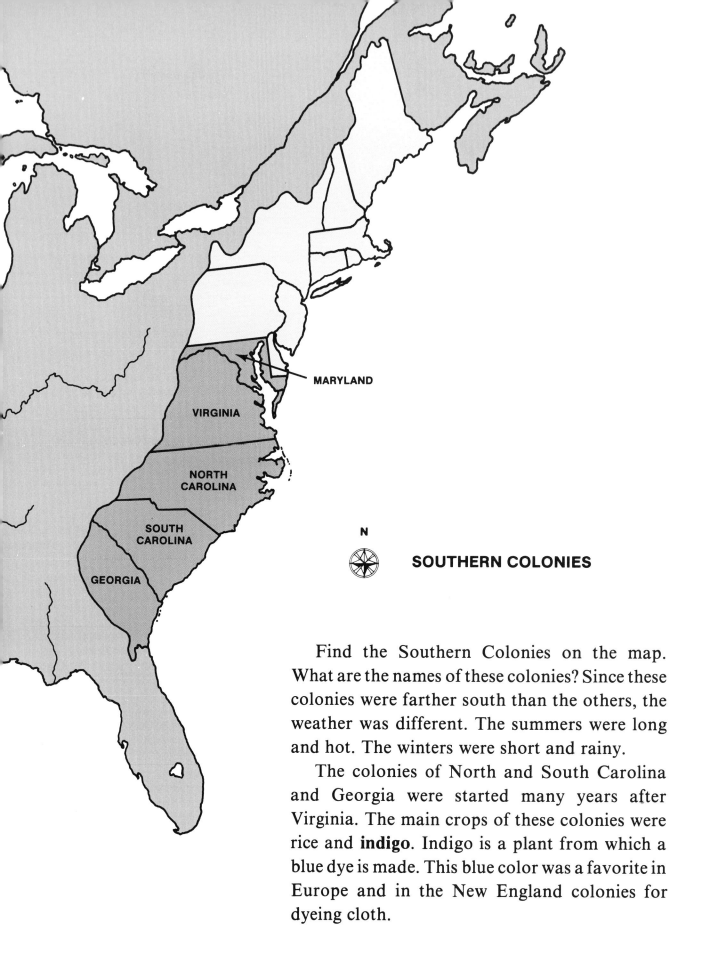

MARYLAND

VIRGINIA

NORTH
CAROLINA

SOUTH
CAROLINA

GEORGIA

N

SOUTHERN COLONIES

Find the Southern Colonies on the map. What are the names of these colonies? Since these colonies were farther south than the others, the weather was different. The summers were long and hot. The winters were short and rainy.

The colonies of North and South Carolina and Georgia were started many years after Virginia. The main crops of these colonies were rice and **indigo**. Indigo is a plant from which a blue dye is made. This blue color was a favorite in Europe and in the New England colonies for dyeing cloth.

Tobacco, rice, and indigo are crops that need a great deal of work in planting, tending, and harvesting. Some men bought great amounts of land to grow their crops, but they could not do all the work alone. They got servants or **slaves** to help them.

Many people were willing to come to America to be servants. A person would promise to work for a master for seven years without pay. In return, the master would promise to pay for the servant's trip across the ocean and to provide food, clothing, and a place to live for the seven years. Then the servant would be freed.

At first only a few of these servants were black. But planters wanted workers in their fields who would work more than seven years. They wanted slaves instead of servants because slaves had to work for the planters for their whole lives. Also slaves could be bought and sold. Many other nations had been using blacks stolen from their homes in Africa. Planters in the American colonies began to use these blacks as slaves too.

It is wrong to make other people slaves. Some people tried to use the Bible to prove that slavery was right. The Bible does not say that anyone should be a slave to any other person.

Slavery continued and grew because men were greedy for money. The Northern Colonies built the ships that carried the slaves. Slave dealers came from almost every colony. Most of the slaves worked in the Southern Colonies.

Slavery continued in America for more than a hundred years. Finally, laws were passed that made all men and women free from slavery.

The owners of the large farms were known as **planters** and their farms were known as **plantations.**

Notice that the plantation is located near water. This was done so that the products could be easily loaded onto ships.

mansion

kitchen

courtyard

office

gardener's house

storehouse

spinning house

flower garden

icehouse

school

greenhouse

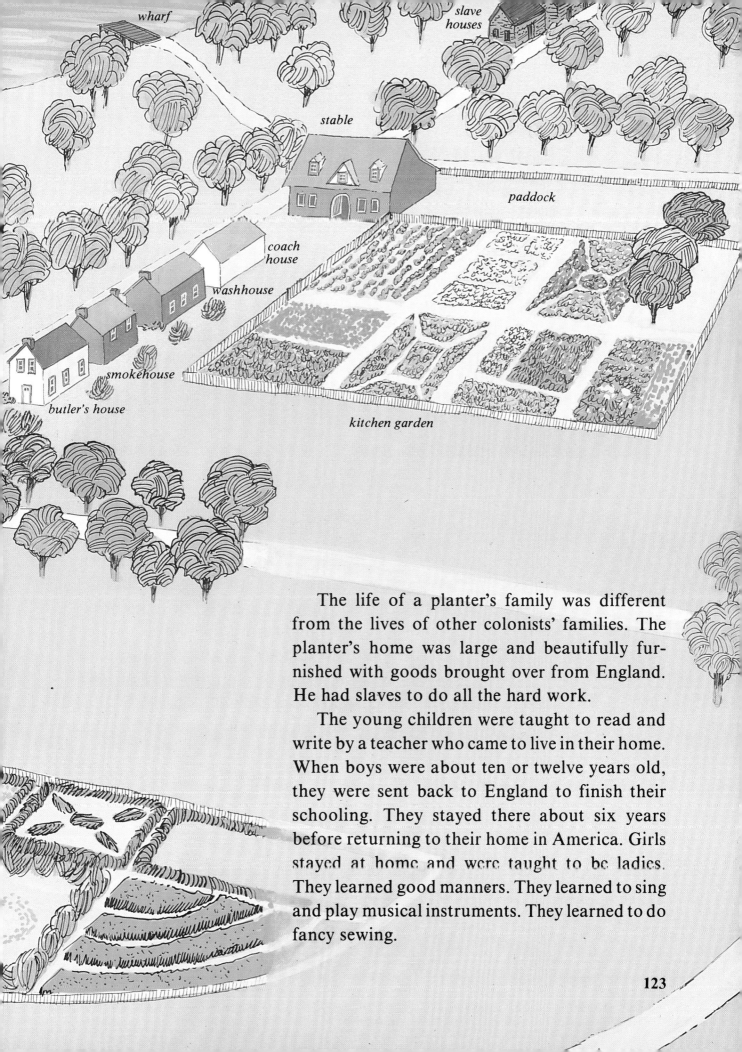

wharf

slave houses

stable

paddock

coach house

washhouse

smokehouse

butler's house

kitchen garden

The life of a planter's family was different from the lives of other colonists' families. The planter's home was large and beautifully furnished with goods brought over from England. He had slaves to do all the hard work.

The young children were taught to read and write by a teacher who came to live in their home. When boys were about ten or twelve years old, they were sent back to England to finish their schooling. They stayed there about six years before returning to their home in America. Girls stayed at home and were taught to be ladies. They learned good manners. They learned to sing and play musical instruments. They learned to do fancy sewing.

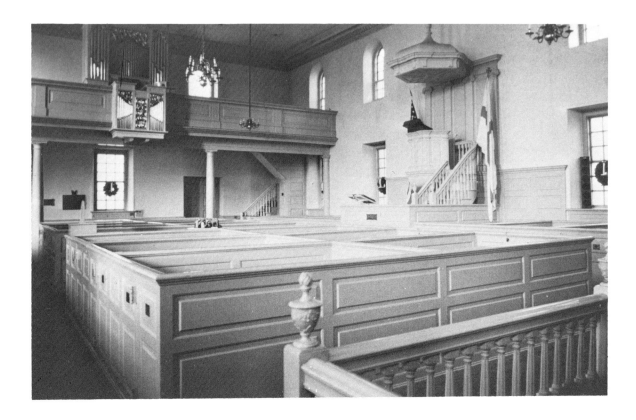

*George Washington attended this church.*

The earliest southern settlers in Jamestown, Virginia, were faithful in attending church. They went whether they wanted to or not. Every Sunday, a half hour before the church service began, guards would search all the houses and force everyone to go to church. Only the sick people were allowed to stay at home.

In later years the laws were not so strict, but most of the colonists attended church anyway. Some were not interested in worshiping God, but they looked forward to this opportunity to see their friends. The churches were usually built by a river so that the people could come in a boat.

Each family had its special pew in colonial churches, and no one else could sit in it. In some churches the pews in the balcony were considered to be the best seats.

Look on the map to find a city called Salem in North Carolina. Salem was built by Moravians. The Moravians were a religious group in Germany. They believed the Bible, and they wanted to live for God. They sent missionaries to Africa and to other parts of the world.

Some Moravian missionaries went to Pennsylvania to preach to both the Indians and the colonists. They built some small towns there. Years later, some of the Moravians from Pennsylvania moved to North Carolina. The Moravians were a peaceful people. The word *Salem* means "peace."

The Moravians believed that their families were very important. They built "little boys' schools" and "little girls' schools." The small children learned to read, write, and work with numbers there.

When the young people were fourteen years old, they left home to live in a "single house." In the "single sisters' house," girls learned to weave, spin, sew, and do other housekeeping jobs. In the "single boys' house," boys learned how to be carpenters, tailors, bakers, shoemakers, or other kinds of workers. The young people were taught to work "with industry, faithfulness, ability, and good behavior." They stayed in the "single houses" until they were married.

The Moravians loved music. Nearly everyone learned to play at least one musical instrument. When a house was built, a trumpeter would climb to the top to play a hymn of thanks. When a harvest was finished, men went into the fields playing songs of thanksgiving. There were choirs for all ages, and they often sang with orchestras of violins.

The church was the center of Moravian life. One of their church services was called a love feast. The people gathered to sing praises to God. During the service, sweet buns and tea or coffee were served. The people enjoyed eating with their friends.

Perhaps the most special church service of the year was the Easter sunrise service. Early Easter morning the people gathered at the church to hear the Easter story read from the Bible. Then the band played while the congregation sang an Easter hymn. Next the people walked outside to a nearby cemetery for the rest of the service. This service helped them remember the Resurrection of the Lord.

The Moravians were good colonists. They were honest and hardworking people. They taught their children what was right. They tried to win the unsaved Indians and white people to the Lord.

Another group of settlers who came into the Southern Colonies was the Scotch-Irish. These were people from Scotland who had lived for some time in the northern part of Ireland. Trouble came to them there. They were persecuted for their religious beliefs. There were also several years of poor crops. Thousands of these people came to America.

Most of the Scotch-Irish came first to Pennsylvania. They soon moved on into the mountain regions of Virginia and Carolina. In Pennsylvania they saw the log cabins that the Swedish and German colonists lived in. They decided to build that kind of home too.

The Scotch-Irish were strong, independent people. They were described as fearing God but nothing else. They were eager to own land, so they fought the Indians in order to get it. They did not do a great deal of farming. Instead they became hunters and trappers.

We call the Scotch-Irish and others who settled the western part of the colonies **frontiersmen**. Perhaps the most valuable possession of a frontiersman was his gun. He needed it to provide food and protection for his family. He also needed it to hunt wild animals. He would then sell the animal skins or trade them for goods that he and his family needed.

The gunsmiths experimented until they had made the famous Kentucky rifle. This rifle was longer than most guns of that time, but it was not as heavy. It was also easier to load and fire.

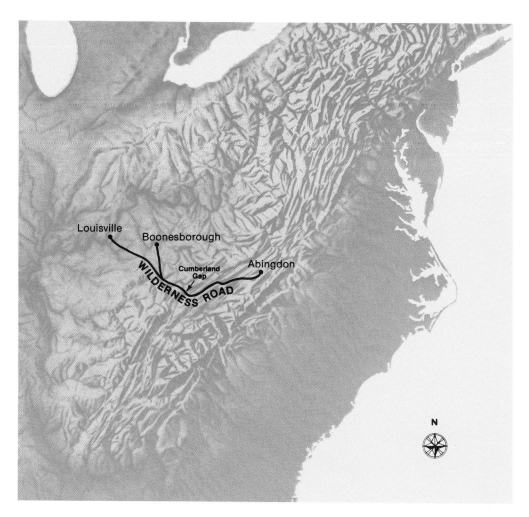

Daniel Boone was perhaps the most famous frontiersman of all. He was the leader of the first group of settlers who took their families into the wilderness to live. He directed the men who cut the Wilderness Road over the Cumberland Gap. This opened the way for other families to move westward.

Daniel Boone never stayed in one place very long. He took many trips to hunt and explore. Once he was gone for two years.

Daniel probably knew more about Indians than any other frontiersman. It was said that he could think like an Indian. Two of his children were killed by the Indians. Daniel often fought against the Indians, but he never hated them.

The colonial towns and cities were small. Notice the signs outside the shops. The pictures were needed because so many people could not read well.

Most colonists lived on small farms, but many boys learned how to be blacksmiths, shipbuilders, carpenters, silversmiths, barrelmakers, or other useful workers. When a boy was about ten years old, he could become an **apprentice** to an experienced worker called a **master**. An apprentice lived in the master's home and worked with him until he learned the **trade**. He often stayed for seven or eight years. The master provided food and clothing for the apprentice. He was also supposed to make sure that the apprentice learned to read and write.

*Ironworker*

*Glassblower*

*Apothecary*

*Printer*

Boys did not always become apprentices to learn a trade. Many learned from their fathers. This was true in the colonies just as it had been in England.

The names of many families came from their trade. A person who worked with iron was a blacksmith, so his family was called the Smith family. The family of a man who ground or "milled" grain would be called the Millers. A man who carved wood was called Mr. Carver.

Here are some names that were taken from the family trade.

| Family Name | Trade |
| --- | --- |
| Wright | made wheels |
| Carter | moved goods on a cart |
| Cooper | made barrels |
| Parker | took care of parks |
| Clark | clerk |
| Carpenter | made things of wood |
| Baker | made bread |
| Chandler | made candles |
| Kellogg | butchered hogs |
| Taylor | made clothing |
| Weaver | made cloth |

After the early colonists came to America, they often thought of their old homes. Many of them made their houses and other buildings like the ones they had left behind. They often gave the new colonies, towns, and cities names that they were used to. New Hampshire and New Jersey are named after places in England. Boston, Massachusetts and New London, Connecticut were named for cities in England.

Many places in the colonies were named to honor kings, queens, or other important people. Some of these are Jamestown, Williamsburg, Maryland, and Georgia.

The names of a few cities came from the Bible. Bethlehem, Pennsylvania, and New Canaan, Connecticut, are examples.

Some place names came from the Indians. The names *Massachusetts* and *Connecticut* come from Indian words meaning "near the great hill" and "at the long river."

As years passed, people who lived and worked in a town did not think about its name. Old people died, and new families moved into town. Names of places usually stayed the same even though the reasons for them were forgotten.

The colonists did not use money as much as we do today. Instead they traded goods they had grown or made for goods and services they needed. A farmer might trade corn to a storekeeper for salt. A fisherman might trade some dried fish to a barrelmaker for some barrels he could pack his fish in. A carpenter might make some furniture for a family in return for some trees he could cut for wood he needed.

The coins the colonists used were called pence, shillings, crowns, and pounds instead of pennies, nickels, dimes, and dollars. Sometimes corn or tobacco was used for money.

They also used a kind of money called **wampum**. Wampum was made from seashells. It was often used in trade with the Indians.

*Wampum*

*Paper money*

*Pine tree shilling*

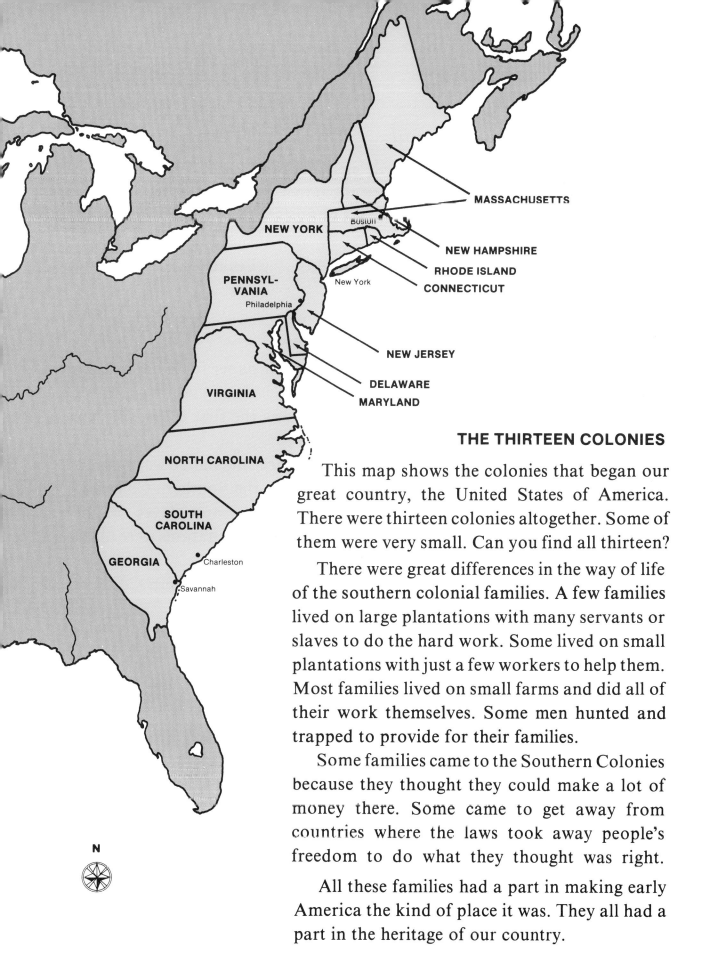

MASSACHUSETTS

NEW YORK

Boston

NEW HAMPSHIRE

RHODE ISLAND

CONNECTICUT

PENNSYL-
VANIA

Philadelphia

New York

NEW JERSEY

DELAWARE

MARYLAND

VIRGINIA

NORTH CAROLINA

SOUTH
CAROLINA

GEORGIA

Charleston

Savannah

N

## THE THIRTEEN COLONIES

This map shows the colonies that began our great country, the United States of America. There were thirteen colonies altogether. Some of them were very small. Can you find all thirteen?

There were great differences in the way of life of the southern colonial families. A few families lived on large plantations with many servants or slaves to do the hard work. Some lived on small plantations with just a few workers to help them. Most families lived on small farms and did all of their work themselves. Some men hunted and trapped to provide for their families.

Some families came to the Southern Colonies because they thought they could make a lot of money there. Some came to get away from countries where the laws took away people's freedom to do what they thought was right.

All these families had a part in making early America the kind of place it was. They all had a part in the heritage of our country.

135

*Praise to God*

"O praise the Lord, all ye nations: praise him, all ye people. For his merciful kindness is great toward us: and the truth of the Lord endureth for ever. Praise ye the Lord."

Psalm 117

**New words**

apprentice
frontiersmen
indigo
master
plantation
planter
slave
trade
wampum

**Things to remember**

Write *yes* or *no* on your paper for each sentence given.

_____ 1. Virginia was the first of the thirteen colonies.

_____ 2. Tobacco, rice, and indigo were important crops in the Southern Colonies.

_____ 3. All the servants and slaves on the large southern plantations were black persons.

_____ 4. Most girls in the Southern Colonies went to school.

_____ 5. Most families in the Southern Colonies lived on small farms.

_____ 6. The buildings on a plantation were usually built close to a river.

_____ 7. The winters in the Southern Colonies were long and cold.

_____ 8. Music was an important part of life in the Moravian city of Salem.

_____ 9. New York was one of the Southern Colonies.

_____ 10. Blue dye is made from indigo.

## Things to talk about

1. Would you like to have lived on a large plantation in colonial days? Why?
2. Would you like to have lived in Salem, North Carolina, in its early days? Why?
3. The main reasons we go to church are to worship God and to praise Him. What are some other reasons we go?
4. Do you think laws should be made that everyone must go to church? Why?
5. What are some ways you and your family use music?
6. Do you plan to play a musical instrument? Which one?
7. Have you ever been to an Easter sunrise service? What was it like?
8. What does it mean to work "with industry, faithfulness, ability, and good behaviour"? Do you work that way?

## Things to do

1. Put the names of the Southern Colonies on your map. Color them light green.
2. Dye some cloth with dye made from a plant.
3. Make a list of good manners that ladies and gentlemen ought to have.
4. Draw a map of the plantation mansion and the buildings around it.
5. Make a list of jobs you could do to help your family.
6. Try to find out how you could learn to be one of these workers: plumber, carpenter, brick mason, mechanic, cook, secretary.
7. Try to find out the meaning of your name.
8. Try to find out when your hometown was started. Where did its name come from?

# 7 The New Nation

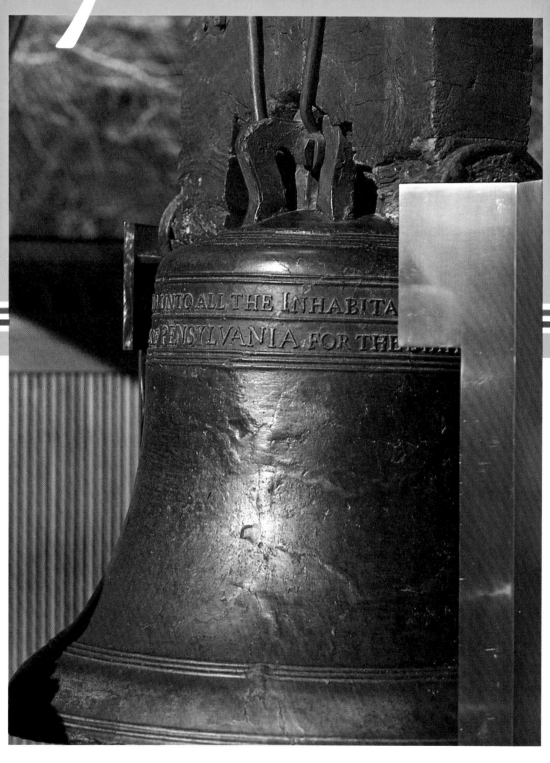

# Goals

1. I will be able to recite the verse that is written on the Liberty Bell.
2. I will be able to tell the reason that we celebrate the Fourth of July.
3. I will be able to tell about the war between the American colonies and England.
4. I will be able to tell about some persons who helped win the War for Independence.
5. I will be able to recognize the Seal of the United States.
6. I will love my country.

This is the Liberty Bell. It is a symbol of freedom. On the bell is written part of Leviticus 25:10. "Proclaim liberty throughout all the land unto all the inhabitants thereof." This bell reminds all who see it of the freedom we enjoy in America. It also reminds us to be good citizens so that our freedom will not be lost.

**Map A**

**Map B**

As the years went by, the thirteen colonies in America grew. Thousands of persons from England, Holland, Germany, France, and other countries came to America to find a new life. They cleared land for farms. They built towns and cities. They were free to worship God as they wished. Many families owned their own homes and had plenty to eat and good clothes to wear.

The families that grew up in America were different from their relatives who stayed in Europe. Their schools were different, their homes were different, their food and clothing were different. Their ideas about what was important were different.

America was a big land, and most of it was wild. The colonists had to work hard to make a living. They had to be brave to face the dangers from Indians and wild animals. There was also danger from unfriendly French and Spanish settlers who lived nearby. The colonists had to have strong character in order to succeed.

These families in the New World knew that the thirteen colonies belonged to England. But they also knew that they wanted to be free men and women. They often called themselves Americans instead of Englishmen.

Look at Map A to see the land claimed by France and England in 1760. Notice that they both wanted some of the same places. They fought a war to decide who would own the land. The king of England sent soldiers to America to fight the French. The French were defeated. Look at Map B to see the land they gave to England.

When George III became king, he decided to have his soldiers stay in the colonies. They had no homes there, so a law was made that ordered the colonists to let the soldiers live with them in their homes. The colonists were even supposed to help pay the soldiers. They did not want to do this, since the war was over.

King George was a proud man who liked to show his authority. He and the English government decided to pass other laws that the colonists would have to obey. These laws took away freedoms that the Americans had enjoyed for many years.

*King George III of England*

The colonists could have ironworks to produce bars of iron, but they were not allowed to make nails. The iron bars had to be sent to England to be made into nails. Then the nails were shipped back to America.

The colonists could weave woolen cloth in their homes. If they made more cloth than they needed, they could not sell it to someone who lived in another colony, even if they were friends. These and other laws seemed wrong to the Americans.

The leaders of the colonies sent messengers to the king. They told him that the Americans thought that the laws were unfair. The king became angry and refused to listen. He sent more soldiers to America. He said that they were there to protect the colonists, but the colonists thought that they could protect themselves.

The soldiers from England were known as British soldiers. Many times they were called "Redcoats," because the coats of their uniforms were red. Some colonists made fun of them and called them "Lobsterbacks."

The colonial children of Boston liked to go ice-skating and sledding just as you do. One winter the British soldiers tried to stop the children's fun by breaking up the ice and spoiling the snow. Several boys got together and went to the British general. They told him what had happened. The general gave orders to the soldiers that they were not to bother the children again.

As time went by, the disagreements between the colonists and the king became worse. By 1775 many Americans had decided that they had better get ready in case there were a war with England. They practiced marching and shooting. Boys in their teens joined with the older men.

They called themselves Minutemen because they would be ready to fight any minute. A group of Minutemen collected a supply of guns and ammunition. They stored these weapons in the nearby towns of Lexington and Concord.

A British general in Boston decided to send some soldiers to destroy the Americans' supplies. The colonists learned about the plans. A brave man named Paul Revere volunteered to go to warn the Minutemen that the British were coming. He left Boston about ten o'clock at night. He rode a borrowed horse to Lexington, awakening people on the way to tell them the news.

When the British soldiers arrived in Lexington the next morning, they were met by a small group of Americans who were ready to fight. Someone fired a shot. The war had begun.

There was fighting all along the way from Lexington to Concord. The British lost many men in the battle that day. Some Americans were wounded and killed too, but the Americans won the victory. Everyone knew that they were willing to fight for freedom.

The wife of an American who died in that first battle wrote these words: "He was then thirty years old. We had four children; the youngest about fifteen months old. The children were sick when he left. As he left the house, he only said, 'Take good care of the children,' and was soon out of sight." The woman never saw her husband alive again.

The colonists often talked about the trouble with England. In May 1775 each colony sent men to a special meeting in Philadelphia. These men met in the building shown on page 164.

The men discussed all that had happened. They agreed that King George III had done things that proved that he was not their king anymore. He had sent thousands of soldiers to America, but they did not protect the colonists. Instead, they had fought against the Americans. Also, the king had told the officers of his navy to stop any ships they wanted to and take all the American goods they could. Besides, the king had even told the officers of his army to persuade the Indians to turn against the colonists and to burn their homes and steal their belongings. A king who cared about his people would not do such things.

Weeks and months went by as the men talked about what the colonies should do. They sent messengers to King George again, asking him to treat them fairly. He still refused to listen.

Finally, John Adams of Massachusetts suggested that the Americans must tell the world that they were not English colonies anymore. He felt that they must take their place in the world as a free nation. Many of the other men agreed with Mr. Adams, but some were still not quite sure.

A committee of five was chosen to write down the reasons they had for declaring that the Americans were free from England. One of the committee members was a young man named Thomas Jefferson. Mr. Jefferson had studied law and had read books about how a country should be ruled. The others decided that he should do the actual writing. Mr. Jefferson spent many days trying to get all the reasons written in the right way. Finally, the committee was satisfied. The paper was called the **Declaration of Independence.**

But still the discussions went on. The men at the meeting knew that they had to make a decision. Should the Americans declare to the world that they were a free nation and would never go back to being colonies again?

A day was set to settle the question. Each colony would get one vote. Caesar Rodney, a man from Delaware, had been called home. John Adams said that they must send for him. They wanted every colony to vote for freedom.

The appointed day was rainy and very warm. The men's tight clothes and heavy wigs made them very hot and sticky. Flies and mosquitoes came in the open windows. They bit the weary men and made them even more uncomfortable. Just after lunch, the men heard the sound of hoofbeats. Mr. Rodney entered the meeting room. He was so weary he could hardly stand. His clothes were covered with mud. He had traveled all night so that he could vote for what he believed was right.

The names of the colonies were called. Twelve voted to declare that they were free. The men from New York decided not to vote until they knew for sure what the people in their colony wanted to do.

Then the Declaration of Independence was read aloud to all the men. They went over it very carefully. They talked about the reasons Mr. Jefferson had written down. They decided that the reasons were right and good.

On July 4, 1776, twelve colonies voted to accept the Declaration as it was written. (On July 9, 1776, the men from New York voted for it too.)

It was done! They had decided. They were free and independent states in America. They would never be colonies again.

In a few days a special copy of the Declaration was made. The men who were still at the meeting signed it. The first man who signed it wrote his name in very large letters. His name was John Hancock.

On July 8, the Declaration of Independence was read aloud to the people of Philadelphia. As soon as it was finished, someone started ringing the bell that hung in the tower of the hall. Bell-ringers in churches all over the city added to the sound. The people began to cheer and shout. Cannons were shot off. People paraded in the streets. Night came and bonfires were lit. Still the bells rang. It was a glorious celebration.

The Americans knew that the Declaration of Independence would make King George more determined than ever to fight against them. They chose George Washington to be the leader of their army. It did not seem that the Americans had a chance. Their army was small. The soldiers were not well trained. They did not have enough food, clothing, or guns. Many times there was no money to pay them. But they were willing to fight!

The war dragged on. The Americans lost some battles, but they did not give up. Many men were killed, but the soldiers did not quit.

The doctors of those days did not have the medicines that are used today. They did not even know about germs. They did not know how diseases spread. Because of this, many soldiers died even though they had only slight injuries. More men died of diseases than were killed by their enemies.

*Prayer before battle as the British approach*

Colonial men were not the only ones who had a part in the war. Women made clothing and prepared food for the soldiers. They set up hospitals and nursed the wounded. They melted their pewter dishes and made bullets from the molten pewter. At home children helped their mothers do the work that their soldier fathers would have done there. Many wealthy families gave their money to buy guns and ammunition for the army.

Finally, in 1781, the last battle was fought. The British were defeated; the Americans had won.

Today, American Christians are proud of those who helped win the War for Independence. We have many freedoms today because of what they did.

The Bible teaches that it is God's will that nations have laws and government. Good laws and good government make it possible for the citizens of a country to live "a quiet and peaceable life in all godliness and honesty" (I Timothy 2:2). King George III and the English government made laws that took away freedoms that the Americans believed God wanted them to have. They were willing to fight for these freedoms.

The stories on these next pages are true. Of course, you know that there were no cameras or tape recorders in colonial days, so we cannot be sure each detail is exactly right.

*Minuteman*

### Patrick Henry

The men at the Virginia Convention did not know what to do. They had talked about it again and again. Their governor seemed to care more about the king of England than he did about his own people of Virginia. Should they oppose him? Would there be war with England? Should they fight if there were a war?

Patrick Henry had thought about the problem many times. He did not believe that the king of England had a right to make the laws for Virginia or any other colony. He thought that the colonies ought to be free even if it meant war.

Mr. Henry made the suggestion that the colony of Virginia should start to raise an army to protect itself against England. Immediately some other men disagreed. They were not at war yet. Why not wait a while longer to see what would happen?

Patrick Henry stood up and looked about at the men. Everyone became quiet as he began to speak. Carefully Mr. Henry reminded the men of the troubles caused by the English laws. One by one, he listed the reasons that proved that they should be ready for war. Finally, he ended his speech by saying, "Our brethren are already in the field! Why should we stand here idle? What is it that the gentlemen wish? What would they have? Is life so dear or peace so sweet as to be purchased at the price of chains and slavery? Forbid it, Almighty God. I know not what course others may take, but as for me, give me liberty or give me death!"

His words convinced the men. The suggestion was accepted, and Virginia prepared for war.

*Peter Salem and Salem Poor*

Peter Salem and Salem Poor were two black soldiers who fought in the second battle of the war. This battle was called the Battle of Bunker Hill.

All night long the Americans worked rapidly to build a wall of earth and rocks around the top of the hill near Boston. In front of the wall, they dug a ditch. When dawn broke, the British saw what had been done. They decided that they would capture the hill and drive the American soldiers from Boston.

In close formation the Redcoats marched up the hill. The American commander ordered, "Don't fire until you see the whites of their eyes." Closer and closer came the British. Then the firing began. The British soldiers fell back, leaving many wounded and dying behind. They reformed their lines and marched back up the hill. Again the American gunfire drove them back.

At one time a British officer appeared suddenly before a group of American soldiers and ordered them to surrender. The men were so startled that they just looked at him and did nothing. Peter Salem leaped forward, shooting as he went. The others, encouraged by his action, began firing again, and the battle continued.

The British made a third try to take the hill. This time the Americans were out of powder, and the British were successful. After the battle, an American general gave special praise to another black soldier, Salem Poor. He said that he had "behaved like an experienced officer, as well as an excellent soldier."

The British won the battle, but they lost almost half of their men. Even though the Americans lost the battle, it was an encouragement to them. They saw that the British army was not as powerful as they had feared.

*Peter Muhlenburg*

"The Bible tells us there is a time for all things. There is a time to preach and a time to pray, but the time for me to preach has passed away. There is a time to fight, and that time has come." With these words, the Reverend Peter Muhlenberg ended his sermon.

The congregation sat quietly, wondering at his words. They remembered that he had often preached to them about the importance of freedom. They knew that he was the chairman of the Committee of Safety for their county in Pennsylvania. They also knew how disturbed he was at the news about the Battle of Bunker Hill. What was he going to do?

Peter Muhlenberg slowly took off his robe and stood before his congregation dressed in his army uniform. He strode down the aisle of the church, looking straight ahead. The people rose to follow. When he went outside, a drum began to beat. The pastor stood still for a moment, looking soberly at his congregation; then he started marching down the street. First one, then another, then dozens of men joined him. By nightfall three hundred men were ready to leave their homes to fight for freedom.

Peter Muhlenberg was one of many pastors who took part in the war with England. Not all of these pastors joined the army. Those that stayed at home encouraged and helped the families of the soldiers. They collected supplies for the fighting men. They cared for the sick and the wounded. They faithfully prayed that God would show mercy to the new, struggling country of the United States and to its people.

*Nathan Hale*

The Rangers stood quietly before their commander. Every eye was upon him. He told the Rangers General Washington's message. The General wanted a volunteer to go into New York to get information about the British. It was a dangerous assignment. At first no one volunteered. Then Nathan Hale stepped forward. He would go. He would find out where the British had their soldiers and ammunition.

Nathan Hale was a strong young man who had been a schoolteacher. He had left that work to join the American army. He was chosen to be a Ranger because he was a brave and clever soldier.

Now Mr. Hale pretended to be a Dutch schoolmaster. He easily crossed the British lines and got the information that was wanted. But then Nathan Hale was captured! Some people believe that he was betrayed by his cousin, who was loyal to the British. He was taken before a British general in New York. The general ordered that he be hanged the next day.

Mr. Hale calmly prepared for his coming death. He asked for a Bible, but his request was refused. He wrote a letter, but it was destroyed. When it was time for him to die, he made a speech to the people gathered around. The last words he said were, "I only regret that I have but one life to lose for my country."

Nathan Hale died a hero and a patriot. He gave his life for what he believed was right.

## Molly Pitcher Hays

Mary Hays wanted to be with her husband, John, when he joined the army to fight against the British. She went with him, cooked for him, and took care of his clothes. John showed Mary how to fire a cannon, and soon she could do it as well as he.

One June day in 1778, the Americans met the British in a battle at Monmouth, New Jersey. It was about one hundred degrees in the sun, and soon the soldiers were suffering from thirst. Mary decided that she could help by being a water carrier. Back and forth she went to a nearby spring, bringing pitcher after pitcher of water to the gasping, exhausted men. They began calling her Molly Pitcher.

Suddenly there was an order to retreat. Retreat? The battle had hardly begun. In the confusion that followed, a cannon was left untended. John Hays ran to the gun and began to fire. Soon he fell, wounded by a British bullet. Soldiers started to drag the cannon to the rear of the battlefield. Mary grabbed the rammer from her wounded husband's hand and began to shoot the cannon. As she was firing, a British cannon-ball went between her legs, tearing off the bottom of her petticoat. Even this did not stop her. She was busy loading and firing the cannon when General Washington arrived at the scene of the battle.

The general gave several quick commands. The soldiers obeyed, and order was restored.

General Washington was pleased with the courage of "Molly Pitcher" Hays. He honored her by making her a sergeant in his army. She then became known as Sergeant Molly Pitcher.

*John Paul Jones*

John Paul was a brave Scottish sailor. He went to sea when he was only twelve years old. By the time he was twenty-two, he was the commander of a ship. Four years later, John Paul added Jones to his name and went to America to live. He returned to the sea when the war with England began. Captain Jones fought in many battles, but he is best remembered for one fought in 1779.

The cannons roared! The gunfire flashed in the darkness! Suddenly two large guns on the old American ship, the *Bonhomme Richard*, exploded. The captain of the British ship, the *Serapis*, saw what happened. "Has your flag been struck?" he asked. Captain John Paul Jones shouted firmly, "I have not yet begun to fight!"

After a time of fierce fighting, the ships collided. The *Richard* tilted sharply. Water poured in through many leaks. Captain Jones ordered sailors to lash the ships together. The *Serapis* tried to pull away, but the ropes held fast. The muzzles of the guns on the two ships touched each other.

By this time most of the guns on the *Richard* were so badly damaged that they would not work. The situation looked hopeless for the Americans.

Then a sailor had an idea. He grabbed a bucket of grenades and climbed the mast of the *Richard*. Carefully he crossed to a mast of the *Serapis*. He looked below him and saw a supply of gunpowder. Without thinking of his own safety, he dropped a grenade into the powder. An explosion rocked both ships. Flames lighted the scene as the terrible battle continued.

After about another hour, the main mast of the British ship was so badly damaged that it could not stand. The British captain knew that he must give up. He hauled down the flag and surrendered to Captain Jones. The Americans were the victors.

The battle was won, but the damage to the *Bonhomme Richard* was great. Two days later the old ship sank.

John Paul Jones served his country faithfully for many years. He is sometimes called "the father of the American navy."

*The Grand Union Flag*

*The Pine Tree Flag*

*The Guilford Court House Flag*

*The Texel Flag*

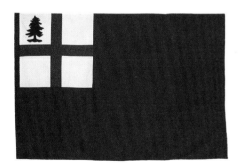

*The Bunker Hill Flag*

*The Gadsen Flag*

*The Flag*

A flag is a symbol. It usually stands for a group of persons who are working together for some purpose. We believe that flags were used during Bible days, because Solomon wrote about an army with banners.

When the thirteen states were still colonies, they usually flew the British flag. But as the trouble between the colonies and King George grew, many colonists wanted a different flag.

In January 1776 the Grand Union was raised by John Paul Jones over an American ship docked in Philadelphia. The stripes represented the thirteen colonies. The cross showed that they still belonged to England.

After the Declaration of Independence was signed, the Americans did not want a flag that had the crosses of the British flag. On June 14, 1777, the decision was made at Philadelphia that the American flag would be "made of thirteen stripes, alternate red and white; that the union be thirteen stars, white in a blue field." Since no requirements were given for the arrangement of the stars, different flag makers made different designs.

In 1818, Congress decided that the flag should always have thirteen stripes to represent the thirteen colonies, but that a star should be added every time another state became a part of the United States.

I pledge allegiance
to the flag of the
United States of America
and to the Republic
for which it stands,
one Nation under God,
indivisible,
with liberty and justice for all.

We must respect and take care of our flag.
1. Do not let the flag get dirty.
2. Do not let the flag get torn.
3. Do not let the flag touch the ground.

This is how to fold a flag.

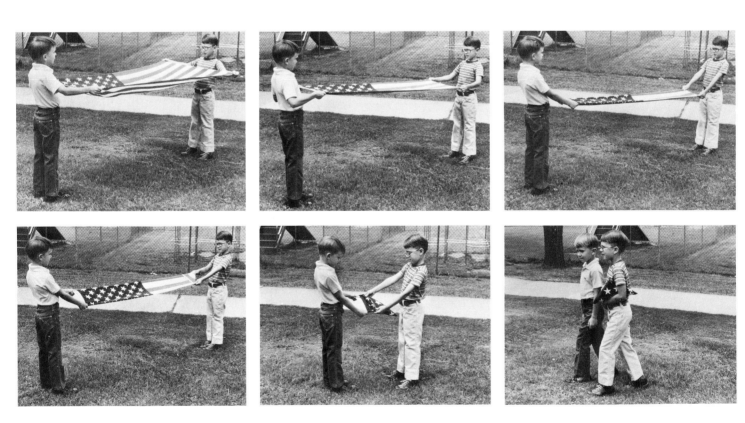

The seal of the United States was accepted by the Congress on June 20, 1782. How many sets of thirteen can you find on the front side? The words on the banner mean "Out of many, One." The olive branch represents power in peace. The arrows represent power in war. The red color represents hardiness and valor. The white represents purity and innocence. The blue represents vigilance, perseverance, and justice.

You can find a picture of the seal of the United States on the back of every one-dollar bill.

## Love for Country

"And ye shall hallow the fiftieth year, and proclaim liberty throughout all the land unto all the inhabitants thereof: it shall be a jubile unto you; and ye shall return every man unto his possession, and ye shall return every man unto his family."

Leviticus 25:10

**New words**

Declaration of Independence

**Things to remember**

Choose a name from this list to answer each question.

George III          George Washington
Nathan Hale          Molly Pitcher
Thomas Jefferson     Paul Revere
Patrick Henry        John Paul Jones

1. Who was chosen to be the leader of the American army?
2. Who wrote the Declaration of Independence?
3. Who was the king of England in 1776?
4. Who said, "I have not yet begun to fight!"?
5. Who carried water to American soldiers during a battle?
6. Who said, "Give me liberty or give me death!"?
7. Who warned the Minutemen that the British army was coming to destroy their supplies?
8. Who said, "I only regret that I have but one life to lose for my country"?

## Things to talk about

1. What could a colonial girl or boy your age do to help win the war with England?
2. A person who loves his country is called a patriot. How can you show that you are a patriot?
3. Describe our country's flag. Tell what the stars, the stripes, and the colors represent.

## Things to do

1. Learn a patriotic song.
2. Design a flag for your class.
3. Draw a picture of one of the persons you read about in the unit.
4. Practice folding a flag correctly.
5. Make a collection of flags or pictures of flags.
6. Make a collection of poems or stories about our flag.
7. Write a poem about the flag.
8. Put on a patriotic program.
9. Draw a picture of the Liberty Bell. Try to find out how it cracked.

# 8 The Constitution

# Goals

1. I will be able to tell what the Constitution of the United States is.
2. I will be able to list the three parts of our government and tell what each part does.
3. I will be able to give the name of the "Father of the Constitution."
4. I will be able to list some rights that are in our Bill of Rights.
5. I will be able to describe some things in the lives of George Washington and Benjamin Franklin.
6. I will obey those who are in authority over me.

The war was over. The soldiers returned home. The people of the thirteen states started thinking about their farms and businesses again. George Washington returned to his plantation in Virginia. He hoped to spend the rest of his life there. But the troubles in America were not over.

During the war, the leaders of the states had written a plan for government. It helped the states work together as they fought against England. But now the plan was not working. The states were not united. Instead they were quarreling with one another. Something had to be done.

The kings in Europe were interested in what was happening in this country. They wondered why George Washington had not made himself the king of America. They did not think that ordinary people knew enough to make a good plan to run a country. They hoped that the states would start fighting among themselves. "If that happens," each king thought, "I will send my army there and take over."

In May of 1787, men from each state came to Philadelphia. They knew that they had to make a plan of government that was good. The states had to work together if the nation were to last. They met in the same building where the Declaration of Independence was signed.

The first thing the men did was to choose a man to be in charge of the meeting. Someone from Pennsylvania suggested that George Washington would be a good leader. A man from South Carolina agreed. No other name was suggested. Each man at the meeting was allowed to write his choice on a slip of paper. When the votes were counted, it was found that George Washington's name was on every slip.

Other officers were chosen. Rules were made for the meeting. A young man named James Madison decided to write down everything that happened. The men were ready for the real work to begin.

*Independence Hall in Philadelphia*

*The room where the Constitution was signed*

The men talked about the nation's problems. At first, some thought that the old plan of government could be fixed to make it better. But finally they all agreed to start over. They would make a completely new plan. It would give less power to each state and more power to the national government.

The discussions went on day after day. The men from the large states did not agree with those from the smaller states. The men from the farming states had ideas different from those of the men in the states that had many businesses. Sometimes men became angry and spoke sharp words to one another. Mr. Washington sat in his place and listened. He was fair to each speaker, but he made sure that the meeting was orderly.

Benjamin Franklin went to almost every meeting. He was more than eighty years old. He was so lame that he could not walk at all. He could not even ride in a carriage because the shaking hurt him so much. Each morning he was put in a large padded chair with poles on the sides. Strong men carried him through the streets to the meeting place.

Mr. Franklin was always cheerful. Often his wise words kept men from losing their tempers.

One day, when it seemed as if the men would never agree, Mr. Franklin said,

How has it happened, Sir, that we have not hitherto once thought of humbly applying to the Father of Lights to illuminate our understanding? In the beginning of the contest with Britain, when we were sensible of danger, we had daily prayers in this room for divine protection. Our prayers, Sir, were heard and they wcrc graciously answered. Have we now forgotten that powerful Friend, or do we imagine we no longer need His assistance? I have lived, Sir, a long time, and the longer I live, the more convincing proofs I see of this truth, that God governs the affairs of men.

Although Mr. Franklin was not a Christian, this story shows that he recognized the power of God.

June passed, and still the meetings went on. The weather was hot, and the men were uncomfortable. Each day James Madison wrote down what was said. Often he made good suggestions.

Finally the plan was finished. It said that the government should be in three parts. There should be a group of men from each state to make laws. They were called the Congress. The plan said that there should be a president and vice-president to make sure that the laws were obeyed. It also provided for courts to be set up. When people disagreed about the laws, the courts were to decide who was right. The plan was called the Constitution of the United States.

No one was completely satisfied with the Constitution, but the men knew that they had done the best they could. George Washington asked if they would accept it. One by one the men in the meeting that day voted, "Yes."

On September 17, 1787, the men met again. The Constitution was read aloud. George Washington took a pen and signed his name. Thirty-nine others did the same.

There was no cheering and no celebrating. The work was not done. The men returned home to persuade the people in their states to accept the Constitution. They made speeches to explain the Constitution. They wrote letters to their friends and put articles in the newspapers.

In a few months each state had accepted the Constitution. They voted for men to make up the Congress. They elected George Washington to be the first president. The new nation finally had a government.

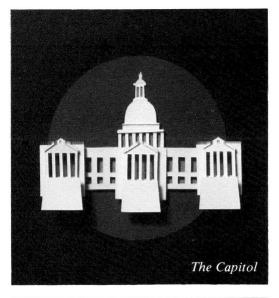

*The Capitol*

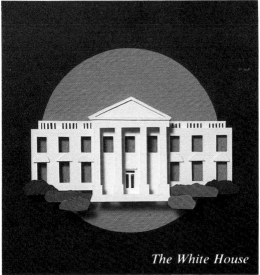

*The White House*

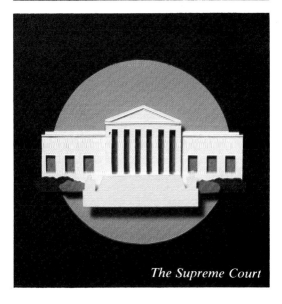

*The Supreme Court*

167

After a time an addition was made to the Constitution. It was called the Bill of Rights.

Americans are thankful for the Constitution of the United States. It was the result of the work of many men. No one had a greater part in making it than James Madison. Because he did so much, Mr. Madison is called "the Father of the Constitution."

Some of the men who helped write the Constitution were Christians; many were not. Even the men who had never accepted Christ as their Saviour believed that there was a God. They believed that men should respect the laws given in the Bible. God used all of these men to give us the best plan of government ever made by men.

## Bill of Rights

Article I
A citizen may believe, say, or write what he thinks is true.

Article II
A citizen may keep firearms.

Article III
The government may not force a citizen to let soldiers live in his home.

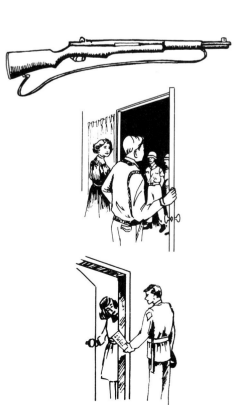

Article IV
No one may search a home without proper permission.

## Article V
The government may not take anything from a citizen unfairly.

## Article VI
Every citizen has a right to a fair trial.

## Article VII
A citizen has a right to a jury trial.

## Article VIII
The government may not torture or unfairly fine a citizen.

## Article IX
A citizen has many rights besides those the Constitution states.

## Article X
The states or citizens have any powers that the Constitution does not deny them or give to the federal government.

*George Washington*

Young George Washington copied the words carefully into the notebook his mother had made for him. The pages contained these words:

Turn not your Back to others especially in Speaking.

Jog not the Table or Desk on which Another reads or writes, lean not upon anyone.

Use no Reproachfull Language against any one neither Curse nor Revile.

Play not the Peacock, looking everywhere about you, to See if you be well Deck't, if your Shoes fit well, if your stockings Sit neatly, and Cloths handsomely.

While you are talking, Point not with your Finger at him of Whom you Discourse nor Approach too near him to whom you talk especially to his face.

Be not Curious to Know the Affairs of Others neither approach those that Speak in Private.

It is unbecoming to Stoop too much to ones Meat. Keep your Fingers clean and when foul wipe them on a Corner of your Table Napkin.

George was pleased with his handwriting. It improved as he practiced each day. He read the words he had written. He knew that they were good rules to follow.

George Washington was glad that he had a chance to go to school. He enjoyed learning. He especially liked mathematics. He always tried to do his problems neatly and carefully. George knew that being able to read, write, and work with numbers would be valuable to him all of his life.

Like most boys, George enjoyed playing games. He could run faster and jump farther than his friends. He liked to play soldier and pretend that he was the leader of an army. Best of all, George liked to ride horses. The faster the horse ran, the more George enjoyed riding it.

George Washington was born on February 22, 1732, on a farm in Virginia. When he was eleven years old, his father died. Then his mother took care of George and his five younger brothers and sisters.

George had an older half-brother named Lawrence, who lived on a plantation called Mount Vernon. George often visited Lawrence at Mount Vernon. There he heard many stories about new lands in the West. He heard about Frenchmen who wanted to take land from the English colonists.

George often thought about going west to explore new lands. When he was about fourteen, he had an idea. He would learn to be a **surveyor**. Then perhaps someone would hire him to go west to measure land.

George found a man to teach him to be a surveyor. He was glad that he had learned mathematics in school. He needed it to do this work. He found some surveying tools that had belonged to his father. Now he was ready for his first job.

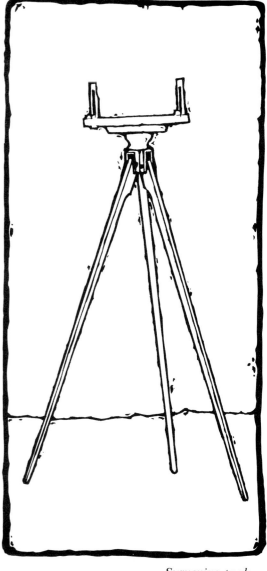

*Surveying tools*

171

When George was sixteen, he was asked to go with some men on a trip west to help measure the land of Lord Fairfax. For a month the men traveled and worked. They rode horseback. They often slept outside. They had to hunt for much of their food. Sometimes they lost their way. It was a hard trip, but George was glad that he had gone. He knew that he had done a good job.

In the next few years, George surveyed land for many men. On each trip he learned more about living outdoors. He also learned how to deal with the Indians.

At this time the English claimed much land in the West. The French claimed some of the same land, and they sent soldiers to hold it. The governor of Virginia asked George Washington to take a message to the French soldiers. The message said that the French soldiers were to leave the English lands.

On November 15, 1753, George and six friends started on the long trip west. They rode horseback for three hundred miles. They crossed mountains and went through valleys. They saw many Indians. George kept a careful record of the entire trip.

Early in December the weary travelers reached the French headquarters. They delivered the governor's message, but the French refused to leave land that they thought was theirs. George and his men started back to Virginia to tell the governor what had happened.

The weather suddenly turned cold, and much snow fell. Because the horses could not travel in the deep snow, George and one other man started walking.

The trip home was long and cold. At one place the men built a small raft to cross a river. Before they were across, large pieces of ice jammed against the raft. George was thrown into the icy water. He saved himself by grabbing onto one of the logs from the raft. Finally, on January 7, they reached home.

George gave the message to the governor. He also drew maps of the land the men had seen. The governor was pleased. He made George a lieutenant-colonel in the army.

In a short time England and France were at war. Washington and his soldiers helped the English army fight in America. During one battle, George had two horses shot out from under him and four bullets went through his coat. But George was not hurt. The war was long, but finally the English won. The French were driven out of the western lands in America.

George learned how to fight in this war. When the war was over, he was the most famous soldier in the colonies.

George Washington returned home. Soon he married a widow, Mrs. Martha Custis. He took his wife and two stepchildren to Mount Vernon. Lawrence had died, and the plantation now belonged to George.

George was a successful planter. He read books to learn all he could about farming. He experimented with new crops. He built flour mills. He directed the work that was done by the weavers, carpenters, bricklayers, blacksmiths, and field-workers who worked on his plantation.

Mr. Washington was a good businessman. He kept records of all the money he earned and spent. He wrote down in his account books the price he received for his crops. He also included the price of his children's toys and his wife's dresses.

The Washington family was happy at Mount Vernon. They lived there for sixteen years. George wanted to spend the rest of his life there. But he knew that there was trouble between England and the colonies. When he was asked to go to Philadelphia to attend a meeting to help decide what the colonies should do, George was willing to go.

In 1775, George Washington was chosen to be the commander in chief of the American army. He was forty-three years old.

*George Washington praying at Valley Forge*

Year after year the war between England and the colonies dragged on. The American soldiers were not well trained. Often they did not have proper food or clothing. Many times the colonists' cause seemed hopeless. But George Washington would not give up. Finally the war was over. The colonies had become the United States of America.

General Washington was happy to go back to Mount Vernon. For about five years he worked hard on his plantation. Then his country needed him again. A good plan of government had to be made.

A huge welcome greeted George Washington when he arrived in Philadelphia. All the bells in the city rang. People crowded near to see the famous general.

General Washington helped write the Constitution of the United States. Then he was chosen to be the first president of our country. After four years, the people voted for him to be the president again.

Finally George Washington returned to Mount Vernon to stay. He was sixty-six years old. He took up his work as a plantation owner again. On December 12, 1799, Mr. Washington was caught in the rain as he rode about his land. He got a sore throat and became very ill. About ten o'clock on the night of December 14, he put the fingers of his left hand on his right wrist. His lips moved as he silently counted his pulse. Then he died.

George Washington was a great American. It was said that he was "first in war, first in peace, and first in the hearts of his countrymen."

*Benjamin Franklin*

"Benjamin," said his father, "I'm sorry, but you cannot go back to school. I need you here at home to help me make candles. You know how to read and write, so you don't need to go to school any longer."

Benjamin was very unhappy. He was ten years old, but he had been in school only two years. He liked learning. His favorite subject was reading. He was interested in finding out about everything. But he knew that he must obey his father.

Benjamin Franklin was born in Boston, Massachusetts, on January 16, 1706. He was the fifteenth of seventeen children. Ben enjoyed playing with his brothers and sisters. He especially liked swimming and boating. He thought he would like to be a sailor when he grew up.

Ben worked in his father's candle shop for two years. Then his father sent him to be an apprentice to his brother James, who was a printer. Ben liked this work very much. He learned quickly and did his work well. He gave up the idea of being a sailor.

Each week James gave Ben money to pay for his meals at a boardinghouse. Ben decided to cook for himself. He spent only half of the money for food. He used the rest to buy books. He read every book he could. Since he could not go to school, he decided to teach himself.

James printed a newspaper. When Ben was sixteen, he wrote some articles that were printed in the newspaper. People who read them praised the young writer.

Ben left Boston the next year. After several days of traveling on foot and by boat, he arrived in Philadelphia. He was tired and hungry. Ben had very little money, but he went to a bakery on Second Street to buy something to eat. First Ben asked for biscuits. The baker did not have any. Then he asked for a three-penny loaf, but the baker did not have one of those either. Finally he asked for as much bread as three pennies would buy. The baker gave him three large, puffy rolls. Ben started down the street eating a roll. He carried the other two, one under each arm.

When Ben came to Fourth Street, he saw a girl standing in a doorway. She looked at him and began to laugh. The girl's name was Deborah Read. Several years later Deborah became Benjamin's wife.

The next day Ben found a job at a print shop. He worked hard and learned more about printing. He made four rules for himself to follow:

1. Save money.
2. Do not promise anybody more than you can do.
3. Do not try to get rich quickly.
4. Do not gossip; instead, speak all the good you know of everybody.

After a few years, Ben opened his own print shop. He printed a newspaper called the *Pennsylvania Gazette*. Many newspapers of that time were made of one page of news from Europe and three pages of advertisements. Mr. Franklin printed local news. He sometimes printed letters that he made up and his answers to them. He even wrote an advice column.

## Of the Eclipfes, 1733.

THIS Year there will be four Eclipfes, two of the Sun and two of the Moon. The firft will be an Eclipfe of the Sun, *May 2.* vifible being about 12 a'clock, Digits eclipfed 2 and a half.

The fecond will be on *May 17.* about two in the Afternoon, wherein the Moon will be eclipfed, not vifible here.

The third will be on *Octob. 26,* about 11 in the Morning, a fmall Eclipfe of the Sun, invifible.

The fourth will be on *Novem. 10,* a little after 6 in the Morning it begins, an Eclipfe of the Moon, above half of which will be darkned.

### *Chronology of Things remarkable,* 1733

*Years fince,*

| | |
|---|---|
| The Birth of JESUS CHRIST | 1733 |
| *Jerufalem* taken by the *Romans* | 1660 |
| Tower of *London* built | 1164 |
| Firft Mayor of *London* | 543 |
| *London Bridge* built with Stone | 524 |
| The Invention of Guns by a Monk | 364 |
| The Art of Printing found out by a Soldier | 293 |
| Great Maffacre in *France* | 161 |
| Spanifh Armada burnt | 145 |
| K.*James* I laid the firft Stone of *Chelfea Coll.* | 124 |
| The Bible new tranflated | 122 |
| Gunpowder Plot | 119 |
| The Plague of *London,* whereof died 30000 | 108 |
| Long Parliament began, *Nov.* 3. 1640 | 93 |
| Rebellion in *Ireland, Oct.* 23. 1641 | 91 |
| King *Charles* I. beheaded | 85 |
| *Dunkirk* delivered to the *Englifh* | 75 |
| *Oliver Cromwell* died, *Sept.* 3. 1658 | 75 |
| King *Charles* II. his Return in Peace | 73 |
| The great Plague of *London,* whereof died 100000, | 67 |
| The great *Seafight* between the *Dutch & Englifh,* | 68 |

One year Benjamin printed an **almanac**. This was a paperback book that told about the weather and gave other useful information. Ben put many wise sayings in his almanac. You may have heard some of these sayings:

Early to bed, early to rise, makes a man
     healthy, wealthy, and wise.

Little strokes fell great oaks.

Keep thy shop and thy shop will keep thee.

Ben pretended that these sayings were by a poor man named Richard. Soon the little book was called *Poor Richard's Almanac.* The almanac was so popular that Ben wrote a new one each year for many years.

Ben worked very hard. Many times he worked until late at night, and he was usually in his shop before his neighbors even got out of bed in the morning. When he had made enough money to keep his family, he gave up his business.

Benjamin Franklin was interested in science. One day a friend showed him some things he could do with electricity. Very few people had even heard of electricity at that time. Ben started experimenting and soon learned new ways to work with that strange power.

Mr. Franklin had the idea that lightning was electricity, and he decided to prove it. He made a kite of two sticks and a silk handkerchief. He fastened a short wire to the top of the kite and a key near the end of the string. He and his son flew this kite during a thunderstorm. At first nothing happened. Then Mr. Franklin held his knuckle close to the key. Just as he had expected, sparks began to fly. This was a dangerous experiment, but it helped him know that his idea was right.

Mr. Franklin continued to study electricity. He discovered a way to protect houses from lightning by using a **lightning rod**. His own house was saved by this invention.

Benjamin learned about other things in science. He studied winds and storms. He learned about the way ants give messages to each other. He studied the movement of water in the oceans. He found a way to make soil better so that it would grow more crops.

Mr. Franklin always tried to be a good citizen. He wanted to make Philadelphia a better city. He helped make laws that required streets to be paved. He planned for a way to light the streets at night. He helped organize fire fighters and a police force. He was responsible for starting a library, a hospital, and a school in Philadelphia. He improved the mail service for all the colonies. He thought of having daylight saving time.

Ben liked to invent things that would help people. He made a stove that did not use much fuel and that warmed homes better than a fireplace. He made the first bifocal eyeglasses. He thought of making a kitchen ladder that folds down into a stool. He did not take any money for the inventions that he made.

*Franklin stove*

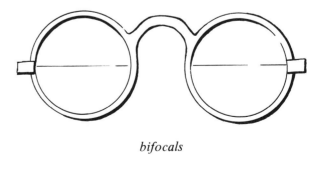

*bifocals*

Benjamin Franklin tried to get the people of the thirteen colonies to work together. He went to England to look after the business of the colonies there. He stayed ten years. When the trouble between England and the colonies became serious, he came home.

In 1776, Mr. Franklin was seventy years old. He gave advice to Thomas Jefferson about what to write in the Declaration of Independence. During the war with England, he went to France to ask for help for the United States.

Mr. Franklin lived in France for several years. The French people loved him. They invited him to their homes. Even the king and queen met with him.

France sent soldiers and ships to the United States to help the new country. When the war was over, men from America and England met in France to sign a peace agreement. Mr. Franklin was one of the men who wrote the agreement.

When Mr. Franklin was eighty years old, he returned to the United States. Crowds of people gathered to meet him. They followed him to his home, cheering as they went.

Benjamin Franklin was old and sick, but his work for his country was not yet finished. He helped make the laws for the state of Pennsylvania. Then he helped write the Constitution of the United States. This was Mr. Franklin's last great service to his country.

Benjamin Franklin died when he was eighty-four years old. He was one of the greatest citizens that the United States ever had.

*Respect for Authority*

"Obey them that have the rule over you, and submit yourselves: for they watch for your souls, as they that must give account, that they may do it with joy, and not with grief: for that is unprofitable for you."

Hebrews 13:17

**New words**

almanac

lightning rod

surveyor

**Things to remember**

Read each sentence. Fill in the blanks.

1. The meeting to make a plan of government for our new nation was held in the city of _____ .

2. The plan of government for our country is called the _____ .

3. The group that makes the laws for our country is the _____ .

4. The first addition that was made to the Constitution was called the _____ .

5. The father of the Constitution was _____ .

6. The first president of the United States of America was _____ .

7. George Washington was born in the state of _____ .

8. George Washington's plantation was called _____ .

9. Benjamin Franklin invented the _____ , _____ , and _____ .

10. Mr. Franklin helped start a _____ , a _____ , and _____ in Philadelphia.

## Things to talk about

1. What does it mean to have freedom of religion?
2. What are some "rights" each person in your class has?
3. What is a citizen of a country?
4. How can children be good citizens?
5. How did George Washington prove he was a good citizen?
6. What do the sayings from *Poor Richard's Almanac* (p. 178) mean to you?
7. It is important for groups of people to have laws.
   a. What are some laws of your town?
   b. What are some laws in your school?
   c. Is it necessary to have laws in a church? Why?
   d. Is it necessary to have laws in a home? Why?

## Things to do

1. Make a list of things you can do to show that you are a good citizen.
2. Make a list of "sayings" you have heard in your family. Tell what they mean.
3. Try to find a modern-day almanac. Does it have wise sayings in it?
4. Think of some laws that you would like to see made.
5. Make a list of things in your home that are run by electricity.
6. Dress like one of your favorite early Americans.
7. Elect a president of your class.

# Glossary

## A

**almanac** a book that contains information about many things, such as the weather, the tides, and the sun, moon, and stars

**apothecary** a person who prepares and sells medicine

**apprentice** a person who learns a trade from a skillful workman

## B

**bay** a wide part of a sea or lake that is partly surrounded by land

## C

**carpenter** a person who builds things of wood

**character** the special way a person acts, feels, and thinks; what a person is really like when he thinks no one is watching

**citizen** a person who is a member of a country; he is either born there or chooses to become a member of that country

**coast** the land along the ocean

**colonist** a person who helps start a colony or who lives in a colony

**colony** a group of people who live in another land but are citizens of their home country

**common** an open field that is used by everyone in the town

**compact** an agreement

**conch** a large spiral seashell

**constitution** the plan of government by which a country or state is ruled

**continent** one of the seven large bodies of land on the earth

**country** the land occupied by a group of people living under the same laws

## D

**down** small, soft, fluffy feathers

## E

**environment** the surroundings in which people, animals, or plants live

**equator** an imaginary line around the center of the earth, halfway between the North and South Poles

**explorer** a person who travels through an unknown place to see what it is like

## G

**garret** attic; space in a house just below the roof

**globe** a map of the earth that is shaped like a ball

## H

**hemisphere** half of the earth

## I

**indigo** a plant from which a bright blue dye is made

**island** a body of land that is surrounded by water

## K

**kachina** the name the Hopi Indians gave to the spirits they believed in

**key** an explanation of the symbols used on a map

## L

**lake** a body of water usually surrounded by land

**legend** a story passed down from person to person; it is usually not true

**lightning rod** a metal rod fastened to a building to conduct lightning into the earth

## M

**maize** the Indian name for corn

**master** a skillful workman

**mesa** a high, flat-topped hill that stands by itself

**moccasin** a soft leather shoe without a heel; first made by the Indians

## O

**oceans** the largest bodies of water on the earth

## P

**patriot** a person who loves and helps his or her country

**pemmican** an Indian food made of dried meat, fat, and berries pounded together

**peninsula** a piece of land attached to a larger piece of land and almost surrounded by water

**pewter** a metal made of tin, copper, and lead

**piki** thin cornbread baked on a flat stone and then rolled

**plain** a large, flat piece of land without trees

**potlatch** a special celebration used by some Indians to show how rich and great they were

**pueblo** an Indian village in which the houses are made of clay bricks and stone and are built close to one another

## R

**river** a large stream of water that flows into a lake, ocean, or other body of water

**role** the part a person has in a family

## S

**sampler** a piece of needlework that is sewn with designs, sayings, alphabet, numbers, or scripture verses

**sassafras** a tree found in the eastern United States; the bark and roots are used for flavoring

**scurvy** a disease caused by a lack of vitamin C

**settler** a person who goes to live in another land

**stocks** a wooden framework with holes for hands or feet, used for punishment

**succotash** a food made by cooking green corn and beans together

**surveyor** a person who measures land

**symbol** something that stands for something else

## T

**tailor** a person who makes clothing

**teepee** an Indian house made by stretching skins over a cone-shaped frame of poles

**totem** a symbol used by some Indians to stand for a tribe, family, or person

**totem pole** a post on which pictures of totems were carved and painted

**trade** a kind of work, especially one that is done with the hands

**trencher** a wooden dish

**tribe** a group of people who come from the same family or who have the same language or customs

## V

**valley** a low place between hills or mountains

## W

**wigwam** a small Indian house made by laying bark or skins over a rounded frame of poles

# Index

# Photo Credits

All photos not otherwise credited are by George Collins.

| | |
|---|---|
| Cover | National Park Service (Richard Frear) |
| p. iv | Unusual Films |
| p. 1 | Robert W. Franklin |
| p. 1 | Richard Peck |
| p. 3 | Unusual Films |
| p. 6 | Unusual Films |
| p. 16 | USAF Photo (363d TRWg) |
| p. 19 | Unusual Films |
| p. 37 | National Park Service (Richard Frear) |
| p. 56 | Metropolitan Museum of Art |
| p. 57 | National Archives |
| p. 58 | National Archives |
| p. 71 | National Archives |
| p. 91 | National Gallery of Art |
| p. 91 | National Park Service |
| p. 93 | National Park Service |
| p. 98 | Unusual Films |
| p. 106 | National Archives |
| p. 120 | National Archives |
| p. 141 | National Archives |
| p. 144 | National Archives |
| p. 154 | National Archives |
| p. 155 | National Archives |
| p. 156 | Library of Congress |
| p. 174 | National Archives |
| p. 175 | National Archives |